MEDITATIVE PRAYER

Entering God's Presence

A SPIRITUAL FORMATION STUDY GUIDE
BY RICHARD PEACE

NAVPRESS
BRINGING TRUTH TO LIFE
NavPress Publishing Group
P.O. Box 35001, Colorado Springs, Colorado 80935

Visit the NavPress web site at: http://www.navpress.com

ISBN: 0-89109-901-8

Cover illustration: Wood River Media, Inc.

Printed in the United States of America

1 2 3 4 5 6 7 8 9 10 / 02 01 00 99 98

CONTENTS

ACKNOWLEDGMENTS...5

HOW TO USE THIS GUIDE...7

INTRODUCTION TO MEDITATIVE PRAYER 11

SESSION ONE
Centering Prayer 15

SESSION TWO
Prayer of Blessing..25

SESSION THREE
Prayer of Worship 35

SESSION FOUR
Meditative Prayer 43

SESSION FIVE
Prayer of *Examen*..53

SESSION SIX
Written Prayers 63

SESSION SEVEN
Prayer of Distress 75

SESSION EIGHT
Prayer Styles and Personality..85

A SELECT BIBLIOGRAPHY 101

LEADER'S NOTES FOR THIS STUDY..102

SPIRITUAL FORMATION STUDY GUIDES
BY RICHARD PEACE

Spiritual Journaling:
Recording Your Journey Toward God

Spiritual Autobiography:
Discovering and Sharing Your Spiritual Story

Contemplative Bible Reading:
Experiencing God Through Scripture

Meditative Prayer:
Entering God's Presence

ACKNOWLEDGMENTS

When it comes to prayer I am such a novice. It seems presumptuous for me to write about prayer. To pray is to delve deeply within and this, for me, is a hard task. To pray is to listen carefully to what we find, knowing that somehow we are in touch with the busy, pulsating spiritual world that surrounds us. Who is up to such a task?

And yet we do pray: weak, halting, inadequate—knowing that God loves us and God hears us and responds to us. What I can offer here is my own experimentation, my struggles to understand, my exploration of the subject via those authors and counselors who are far wiser than I when it comes to prayer. In *Reflections on the Psalms*, C. S. Lewis begins by confessing that he is no scholar of Hebrew, no ancient historian. He writes for the unlearned as one who is unlearned. He goes on to comment that this may not be such a problem after all, because the expert has long since forgotten what troubles the beginner. It is beginners who can help other beginners. I suspect it is my own struggle with prayer that has kept me exploring this subject for so many years. Had prayer been easy, I would not have needed to read so much or struggle so hard.

Various books useful in preparing this material are listed in the notes at the end of each chapter. Four were of special importance. The rich collection of prayers selected by George Appleton and published in *The Oxford Book of Prayer* was invaluable. I recommend it strongly to everyone. Richard Foster's *Prayer: Finding the Heart's True Home* gives a fine overview of prayer styles, and the Michael and Norrisey book, *Prayer and Temperament*, is the focus of session eight. André Louf's *Teach Us to Pray* is as good a discussion of prayer as I know. Derek Kidner's two-volume commentary on the Psalms and the three-volume Word Bible Commentary series on the Psalms also were useful tools.

I am grateful to various people who have assisted me in the production of this book. My wife, Judy, is always present in my writing. Unlike me, she has known how to pray since childhood. And I am grateful for the gentle counsel of Father John Kerdiejus, S. J., whose love and guidance finally enabled this book to be written after a year of struggle.

How to Use This Guide

Introduction

It is preposterous for us to suppose that we can talk to the God of this universe. What a bizarre idea! And yet, in Scripture this is exactly what we are invited to do, over and over again. Prayer is not a minor idea tucked into the cracks of the text. It is central, assumptive, normative. Still, this does not remove the mystery from the endeavor. Human beings—individual men and women—speaking to God and expecting that God not only hears them but responds to them: who can understand such a thing? And who would expect that such an encounter could be straightforward and definable?

Yet we can learn to pray. The disciples asked Jesus, "Lord, teach us to pray," (Luke 11:1). And he did. So, too, we ask, "Lord, teach us to pray" because we know that for us "the first and most fundamental truth about prayer is to know that we are unable to pray," as André Louf puts it.[1] We learn to pray from a variety of sources: from Scripture, from wise men and women who have gone before us, from one another, from our own unfolding experience. This is what this book is all about—a collection of Bible studies, readings, exercises, and small group experiences that are intended to assist us in our ability to pray.

Not that we will ever reach any perfection in prayer. It will always be a challenge—difficult with periods of ease. In the end, we have to keep remembering that prayer is a gift from God. The God to whom we pray gives us our prayers. God gives us the desire and the will to pray. And God gives us prayer so deep that it is known only as groans and longings generated by the Holy Spirit (Rom. 8:22-27).[2]

What's it all about?

Meditative prayer is a term that describes various ways to come to God other than with prayers of intercession. This guide will help you learn these styles of prayer. You can use this guide for a personal journey of prayer, but it is ideal for exploration with a small group of likeminded friends.

Who is it for?
Anyone who longs to pray better, who wants to explore ways to pray that go beyond intercession (asking God for things), and who wants to learn how to use Psalms as a means of spiritual growth will benefit from this course.

What will I learn?
You will learn ways of prayer that include centering prayer, prayers of blessing, the prayer of *examen*, the prayer of confession, and prayers of thanksgiving. You also will learn how the Psalms are used in prayer. Finally, you will explore certain issues that confront us when it comes to prayer, such as finding the right style of prayer, finding time for prayer, hearing God in prayer, using written prayers, and praising God in prayer.

Is this guide only for church goers?
No—although this is written from the vantage point of Christian spirituality, anyone can use this material. All that is required is a sincere desire to pray. There is very little theological language in the course. In the Bible study sections, the background of the text is explained so no knowledge of the Bible is necessary.

How long will it take to go through the book?
The book contains material for eight small group or individual sessions that you will use, ideally, once a week. In addition, there are individual exercises for practice between sessions.

There are two types of sessions. Six sessions focus on learning various prayer styles, and the other two sessions focus on using the Psalms in prayer. These sessions are ordered in the book according to the kind of prayer they address. If time is a problem, you may want to study just the six prayer styles (all sessions but two and seven).

As an alternative, you could meet every other week, or if you're working on your own, you can dip into the book as you have time.

What will a group do for me that I can't get on my own?
Most of us learn new spiritual skills best in the company of others. Small groups allow us to draw upon the combined wisdom, experience, and skills of others. Groups also motivate us.

How can I do the exercises without a group?

If you are working on your own, one option is simply to omit the questions that are designed for reflection or discussion. However, a better option is to buy a notebook and begin keeping a journal of your prayer life. Answer the reflective questions in your journal. If you already keep a journal, you might plan time once a week for prayer and journaling about prayer.

How long does each session last?

If you are meeting with a group of four to ten people, ninety minutes per session is best, but if necessary you can do a session in sixty minutes.

If you are working on your own, you may need less time if you omit the reflection/discussion questions. However, you may need a full hour if you decide to write answers to the reflective questions in a journal.

But I already know how to pray, so why use this guide?

This guide will stretch you in new directions when it comes to prayer. The focus is on less familiar forms of prayer, especially forms that have nurtured Christians in past generations. Prayer is such a vast subject. There is always more to learn, more to experience. In a group, those who are experienced can help the novices.

Who leads the meetings?

Anyone can be the leader. The small group leader's notes at the end of this book (pages 102-111) contain tips on leading, including specific instructions for each session that describe what the leader needs to do. As in any endeavor, the more experience the better. If you have an experienced small group leader in your group, take advantage of his or her skills.

What kind of commitment is needed?

Each person needs to be open to prayer and willing to work at learning new ways to pray. Some groups also may decide to ask members to work on a prayer exercise between sessions and share the results with others in the group.

What happens to the group when it finishes this book?
In session eight you will find various suggestions for continuing as a group, including the use of another book in the Spiritual Formation Study Guides series (see page 4).

A small group covenant
The best way to launch any small group is with clear and agreed-upon expectations. While you may wish to add others, the following commitments are a good place to start.

❖ *Attendance*: I agree to be at the session each week unless a genuine emergency arises.

❖ *Preparation*: I will do the daily prayer exercises as I am able and will share with the group some of what I am learning and what God is saying to me.

❖ *Participation*: I will enter enthusiastically into group discussion, experiences, and sharing.

❖ *Prayer*: I will pray for the members of my small group and for our time together. I will make prayer a priority.

❖ *Confidentiality*: I will not share with anyone outside the group what is said during group sessions.

❖ *Honesty*: I will be forthright and truthful in what I say.

❖ *Openness*: I will be candid with the others in appropriate ways, and I will allow others freedom to be open in ways appropriate to them.

❖ *Respect*: I will not judge others, give advice, or criticize.

❖ *Care*: I will be open to the needs of each other in appropriate ways.

Notes
1. *Teach Us to Pray* (Cambridge, MA: Cowley Publications, 1992), p. 2.
2. The Bible generally uses masculine language (and occasionally feminine terms) when speaking of God. This is not, of course, to imply gender but to indicate personhood. An increasing number of Christians are offended by strict masculine language (knowing that the God of the Bible is not male or female). Others are offended by gender-neutral language. I have chosen to use traditional masculine pronouns on those occasions when they are required, but I recognize that God is not male and that the English language is deficient at this point.

INTRODUCTION TO MEDITATIVE PRAYER

I use the term meditative prayer to describe those ways of prayer that call us to use our minds and imaginations actively as we seek to open ourselves to God's presence. Meditation is different from contemplation. Contemplation involves letting go of all conscious mental and physical activity so as to rest in God's presence, which is a place without form or image. Meditation, on the other hand, is active, involving words, images, and activities. For most Americans, contemplation as defined here is a difficult state to achieve, whereas meditation is a way to relate to God that we can learn and use easily.

This way of relating is not new, though it may feel new to us. We have too long been handicapped in our spiritual growth by too narrow a horizon regarding spiritual practices. We have a kind of collective amnesia, forgetting practices that nourished countless followers of Christ in centuries past. Rediscovering these practices is one way to respond to our culture's deep spiritual hunger. Therefore, I draw upon ancient ways of spirituality.

Assumptions
Several assumptions lie behind the exercises in this guide.

❖ I assume that those who use this guide have had some experience of prayer. This will not be the first time they have prayed. In fact, some may have had years of experience in prayer—in corporate worship, privately on a daily basis, or with others in formal or informal groups.

❖ But I also assume that this prayer experience has been confined mostly to certain types of prayer: intercessory prayer, pastoral prayer during worship, and congregational in prayer unison.

❖ I assume that for most of us it is easier to learn to pray and to practice prayer in the company of others. A small group is a rich laboratory in which to learn new ways to pray and to find new motivation to pray. Hence, the eight sessions of this guide are ideally suited for use in a group of four to ten people. However, they are easily adapted for individual use. (Groups smaller than four will also work; groups larger than ten may want to divide into subgroups of five or six each.)

❖ I assume that we also need to build upon the motivation we find in the small group and so to pray on our own as well. Thus, each session includes individual exercises to use between group sessions. If you are using this guide on your own, you can pace the exercises at whatever speed you choose.

❖ I assume that we all struggle with prayer—if not now, certainly in the future. The struggle itself is from God and part of what we need to learn about the spiritual life.

Some Reflections on Prayer

The prayer exercises should help you to broaden your sense of what prayer is and how to go about it. But the exercises are *not* an end in themselves; they are a means to an end. Nor is prayer even an end in itself. It, too, is a means. The end is contact with God. Prayer is about being open to God. It is not about saying certain words in certain ways. It is not about feeling, thinking, or acting in a certain way. Prayer is the word we use for the ways we open ourselves to the living God.

The problem in prayer is not with God; it is with us. Prayer is not a matter of waking up God or making God pay attention to us. God is always with us, in us, around us, under us, over us. God's presence pervades the universe. And that presence is personal. God loves each of us all the time.

The problem has to do with us and our ability to quell the noise that goes on constantly in our minds. You will discover the pervasive nature of that noise the moment you begin to pray.

❖ There is the noise of need: I'm feeling tired. Or, Why can't I get this project done?

❖ There is the noise of our body: This chair is uncomfortable. Or, I feel tired.

❖ There is the noise of relationships: How long is he going to stay mad at me? Or, I wonder if I should invite Aunt Edna over for Thanksgiving?

❖ There is the noise of pain and problem: How am I going to pay all the bills? Or, I wish I felt better.

So we need to learn to focus on God, to rest in God, to listen to God. Prayer is all about getting through the barriers that keep us from God. The bad news is that this war against noise is never finally won (at least for most of us). The good news is that we can and do win many skirmishes. We can learn to be open to God. In the end, it is God who does the praying. God enfolds us in his love and care in ways that connect with our deepest needs and our deepest wishes.

The fundamental attitude we need to bring to this experience is that of the disciples when they asked, "Lord, teach us how to pray" (Luke 11:1). Unless we know that we do not know how to pray, we will not be open to learning. It is not that we have not prayed nor that we have not grasped the process of reaching out to God. What we need to know is that at a fundamental level, prayer is a mystery. What we know about prayer is minute compared to what there is to know. What we grasp is only the outer fringes of the reality because in prayer we brush against the infinite God of the universe.

The ideal environment in which to learn to pray is a silent retreat at a monastery or conference center where we go for a weekend (or longer). There, in the silence and the structure, we are freed from all the normal diversions and responsibilities that make prayer so difficult. At first the long blocks of silence weigh heavily on us. But gradually we go deep into that silence and find our place of reflection and prayer. At a retreat center we also are helped by the regular services of prayer that punctuate a monastic day and by the opportunity to see a spiritual director.

A small prayer group that meets weekly is another fine environment in which to learn to pray.

The emphasis in this course will be on prayer that is the product of study and reflection rather than on spontaneous prayer. Both types of prayer are needed, but we tend to have more opportunity for spontaneous prayer than we have for reflective prayer. You will find that as you study the prayers of others and as you write your own prayers based on your study of the Bible, your spontaneous prayer will become richer, deeper, and more focused.

One aim of this guide is for each person to develop a regular way of praying that fits who he or she is. In trying out the various options for prayer, stay alert to those that connect most deeply with who you are. When you have tried them all, reflect on which ones you want to use on a daily basis. And don't be intimidated by the concern that you might not be "doing it right." There is no "right way" when it comes to prayer. Prayer methods simply lead us to God, who is the focus of prayer, so experiment until you find ways to pray that fit you.

Centering Prayer

A WAY TO FOCUS ON GOD

Group Note:
Leader's Notes for this session can be found on page 103.

Overview
We want to pray. But whenever we start, we get bogged down. In this first session we will deal with the question of how to begin to pray. The first part of the session focuses on the mechanics of prayer: the *why*, *what*, and *how* of prayer. The second part focuses on centering prayer as a way to begin praying.

Pray the following prayer aloud (if you are meeting with a group, pray in unison):

O God, we (I) long to know you. We long to experience your presence in our lives. Help us in the weeks ahead as we explore together the topic of prayer. Teach us to pray. Give us the motivation we need to pray. Give us the prayers you want us to pray. We pray in Jesus' name. Amen.

OPEN   **20-30 MINUTES**

Prayer

Each of us brings to this small group our own experiences of and assumptions about prayer. What role has prayer played (or not played) in your life so far?

1. Introduce yourself to the group by briefly describing the world in which you live:

   a. who you live with

   b. what you do with most of your day

   c. how you nurture the spiritual side of your life

2. When it comes to prayer, what is your longing?

3. Pick one of the following topics and share your answer with the group:

   ❑ a great experience of prayer you have had

   ❑ an answer to prayer (for you or for someone else)

THE MECHANICS OF PRAYER   15-25 MINUTES

A Prayer Inventory

Take a moment and complete the following prayer inventory. Then, if you are meeting with a group, share your preferences and experiences with one another. If your past experience of prayer is minimal or random, feel free to say so, because everyone is in the group to learn about prayer, starting from wherever he or she might be.

4. *Time*: What time of day works best when it comes to prayer?

   ❏ morning   ❏ evening
   ❏ mid-day   ❏ late at night
   ❏ afternoon   ❏ various times
   ❏ odd free moments   ❏ other:

5. *Place*: Where is it easiest for you to pray?

   ❏ indoors   ❏ outdoors
   ❏ at home   ❏ at work
   ❏ at a desk   ❏ in a chair
   ❏ in church   ❏ other:

6. *Posture*: How do you best pray?

   ❏ sitting   ❏ standing
   ❏ kneeling   ❏ walking
   ❏ with eyes open   ❏ with eyes closed
   ❏ hands folded   ❏ hands raised
   ❏ hands in no particular position

7. *Setting*: What context is best for you to pray in?

   ❏ alone   ❏ with one other person
   ❏ with the family   ❏ with a small group
   ❏ as part of a congregation ❏ other:

8. *Length*: Beyond what point is it difficult for you to pray?

❑ after a few minutes   ❑ after fifteen minutes
❑ after __ minutes   ❑ the moment I decide to pray
❑ it depends on the day   ❑ it's usually easy to pray
❑ it's usually difficult   ❑ other:

9. *Aids*: Which tools, if any, help you to pray?

❑ a Prayer Book   ❑ a book of prayers
❑ a list of prayer requests ❑ a passage of Scripture
❑ none   ❑ other:

In your journal or with your group, discuss what changes, if any, you would like to make in the above six areas that will assist you in prayer.

AN INTRODUCTION TO CENTERING PRAYER   5 MINUTES

When we begin to pray it is often difficult to focus our thoughts. Our minds wander to other things; we feel pressure to "get on with our tasks"; we grow anxious or cautious or hesitant or even fearful. Getting started may be the biggest impediment to prayer.

A good way to move beyond such distractions is to use centering prayer. In this form of prayer, we repeat over and over a few words or phrases, timing these to our breathing. For example, the most famous of such prayers is the so-called Jesus Prayer: "Lord Jesus Christ, have mercy." As you inhale pray, "Lord Jesus Christ." As you exhale pray, "Have mercy." If you keep this up for a few minutes you will find that you are focusing on God and the process of prayer.

While you are praying the Jesus Prayer, open yourself to God. Let go of all other distractions. Ask God to be present, to deal with the distractions, and to give you the prayers you are to pray. Yes, you can pray on several levels simultaneously, repeating a centering prayer while offering other prayers to God.

You may find it helpful to imagine yourself in a place that is holy or special to you: in a garden, a room, or a chapel. For a time, when I was working on the passage in John 4 where Jesus has a conversation with the Samaritan woman, I found it helpful to picture myself actually in the spring of living water about which Jesus speaks (John 4:13-14)—immersed in the life-giving water of the Holy Spirit.[1]

One more comment. Some people are nervous about the idea of repetitive prayer, fearing that this might lead to a "magical" view of prayer in which prayer becomes a kind of mindless mantra. In fact, centering prayer is far from this. It is not mindless. Rather, it helps us focus our minds on God. Nor is it mechanical, as if we catch God's attention through repetition. In fact, centering prayer grounds us in the reality of who God is. Finally, centering prayer is not to be regarded as an end in itself. It is the entrance into other forms and styles of prayer.

PRAYER EXERCISE   20-25 MINUTES

10. Examine the following examples of centering prayers. Some of these have been used through the ages; others have been written by people like you.

   ❑ "Lord Jesus Christ, have mercy." (The Jesus Prayer: seven syllable version.)
   ❑ "Lord Jesus Christ, Son of God, have mercy on me, a sinner." (The longer version with seven syllables followed by eight syllables, which can be used with two breath cycles)
   ❑ "God, have mercy on me, a sinner!" (Luke 18:13)
   ❑ "Come, Lord Jesus, come." (the Maranatha Prayer)
   ❑ "O God, make haste to help me."
   ❑ "Come Lord Jesus, be my guest."
   ❑ "Jesus, let me feel your love."
   ❑ "Lead me, Holy Lord."
   ❑ "Show me your way, Lord Jesus."
   ❑ "Jesus, lead me into joy (or peace, patience, and so on)."
   ❑ "Holy God, bring me your joy (or love, peace, and so on)."

11. Notice the three characteristics of centering prayers.

   ❑ They are short—seven or eight syllables long. The first three or four syllables are prayed as you inhale; the others as you exhale.
   ❑ They include a name for God: "Holy Lord," "Lord Jesus," "Holy Spirit."
   ❑ They end with a request: "give peace," "bring joy," "have mercy."

12. Discuss these characteristics with your group or in your journal.

   a. What names might you use to address God? Try to list as many possibilities as you can in a few minutes. Include names for all three members of the Trinity.

   b. What requests might you make as you seek to focus on God in prayer?

20

13. Take five minutes on your own to write a centering prayer. Don't be afraid to write two or three until you get one that feels right. And don't be afraid to use one of the examples above. Creativity is not the issue; "rightness" for you is the only question. Ask God to lead you.

14. If you are meeting with a group, share your centering prayer with the group.

15. Pray your centering prayer. Spend four minutes in silent meditation, using the centering prayer you have written. (If you are praying on your own, consider using a kitchen timer to mark the four minutes so you don't have to think about the time. Be sure to use a timer that doesn't make noise until the time is up. If you are meeting with a group, you can use a timer, or the leader can let the group know when four minutes are up.)

16. Discuss this prayer experience in your group or journal.

    a. What was the experience of centering prayer like for you?

    b. How might you use this in your own times of prayer?

If you are meeting with a group, let the leader close the session with a brief prayer.

REFLECTION
Unceasing Prayer
It may seem odd to address the issue of unceasing prayer when we are wrestling with how to begin praying. Yet the two issues are connected. The same type of prayer that we use as we seek to "pray without ceasing" is the kind of prayer that enables us to focus on God as we start to pray each day. In both cases centering prayer brings the desired result.

Concerning the value of centering prayer for focusing our minds Theophane the Recluse wrote, "Thoughts continue to jostle in your head like mosquitoes. To stop this jostling you must bind the mind with one thought, or the thought of One

21

only. An aid to this is a short prayer, which helps the mind to become simple and unified."[2]

We can understand why centering prayer (or breath prayer, as it is sometimes called) helps us focus our thoughts on God as we seek to pray. But what about this other use: unceasing prayer? Unceasing prayer does not seem to be a realistic hope for most of us. And yet, the apostle Paul urges us to "pray without ceasing" (or "pray continually" as the New International Version translates this phrase in 1 Thessalonians 5:17). In Romans he says, "Continue steadfastly in prayer" (Romans 12:12 NKJV). In Colossians he says, "Continue earnestly in prayer" (Colossians 4:2 NKJV). It is not just Paul who says this sort of thing. The writer to the Hebrews urges, "Through Jesus, therefore, let us continually offer to God a sacrifice of praise—the fruit of lips that confess his name" (Hebrews 13:15). And Jesus tells the disciples that "they should always pray" (Luke 18:1). Unceasing prayer is not just an afterthought in the New Testament.

This strikes most Christians as an impossible command to obey. How can we be in constant prayer and do anything else in life? We chalk this up as one of those commands that gives us a goal toward which to move but which we know we will never reach. (This is probably an accurate interpretation of these texts.)

Yet some people have taken this command literally. In the fourth century A.D., the desert monks developed the idea of breath prayer as a way of unceasing prayer. In the sixth century, the Jesus Prayer emerged in Eastern orthodoxy. Brother Lawrence, a lay member of a monastic order in Paris in the 1600s, sought to live his life constantly in the presence of God. He learned how to pray in all circumstances, even while washing dishes where he worked. In the nineteenth century, a Russian Orthodox monk prayed the Jesus Prayer until it moved from his mind into his heart and then into his whole body so that eventually the prayer was with him constantly, whether asleep or awake. His story is told in *The Way of a Pilgrim*, a book that has influenced countless people. Nearer our own time, both Thomas Kelly, the Quaker mystic, and Frank Laubach, the missionary educator who taught thousands of people to read and write, told of their pursuit of the continual presence of God.

But what about the repetition of the same prayer over and over again? Is this not the sort of "vain repetition" against which Jesus warned us (Matthew 6:7, KJV)? It is helpful to notice that in the passage where this phrase occurs, Jesus had a very specific problem in mind: those religious leaders who prayed loudly in public and in this fashion drew attention to themselves and their piety.

Jesus then goes on to commend prayer done in secret. This is the character of centering prayer—it is a private, not public, form of prayer. Jesus said, "Do not keep on babbling like pagans, for they think they will be heard because of their many words" (as the more modern New International Version renders Matthew 6:7). The problem in this passage has to do with a magical view of prayer: "If I say it just right and say it over and over again then the incantation will work." This is hardly the Christian view of prayer and certainly not the aim of centering prayer. It is interesting that the next passage in Matthew contains the so-called Lord's Prayer (the "Our Father"), which has been repeated over and over through the ages by countless Christians (Matthew 6:9-13). So repetition does not seem to be the issue. The issue is a sound view of prayer and a humble view of oneself that will not allow the practice of prayer to become a public display of personal piety.

Who knows? Our use of breath prayers as a means of centering may lead us into the place where prayer, if not unceasing, is certainly a throbbing base note that moves mysteriously at the foundation of our daily life and activity.

WEEKLY EXERCISES

Each day: Use the centering prayer that you have been given to start your prayer time each day. Do not be afraid to alter this prayer so that it reflects who you are before God and what you struggle with at that moment in time.

Day one: Finding time. Experiment with different times for prayer (unless you have found one time period that works well for you). Try praying brief prayers in odd, open moments. One suggestion is to set up triggers to remind you of prayer. Every time you see a robin (or a sunset, clock, and so forth.) turn your mind to God. Or let a certain color remind you to pray. Or choose a certain activity (like taking a shower), sound (a car horn), or situation (a client comes to your desk).

Day two: Finding a place. Where do you pray or where will you pray? The right place is important. Find a place where you are drawn to prayer. For some, the issue of place is more a matter of convenience than anything. Where can I go where I will be undisturbed for the period of time I have set aside to pray? For others, the issue of place is more a matter of spirit and tone. Where can I find the kind of atmosphere that moves me to prayer? Many people find they need a place where the only thing they do is pray. Find your place.

Day three: Finding the right posture. If you pray with your eyes open, try praying with them closed. Experiment with hands folded and hands raised. Try praying while walking.

Day four: Finding useful aids. Get a prayer book from church or buy a book of prayers and see if this helps you pray. A good place to start is with *A Diary of Private Prayer* by John Baillie. Even though it is nearly fifty years old, it is still in print and still valuable to many people.

Day five: Finding a routine. Remember that all of the above are merely suggestions. Do not let all this good advice get you down as you struggle to pray each day! Try to pray for five minutes, knowing that God is honored and you are refreshed. Let your prayer life unfold in ways that are natural to you.

Notes

1. For more about the process of centering, see *Contemplative Bible Reading: Experiencing God Through Scripture* (in this series), pp. 36-40.
2. Quoted by Richard Foster in *Prayer: Finding the Heart's True Home* (San Francisco: HarperSanFrancisco, 1992), p. 124. Foster has an excellent discussion of breath prayer, including a very useful section on writing your own breath prayer (pp. 119-129).

Prayer of Blessing

The *Berakah*

Group Note:

Leader's Notes for this session can be found on page 106.

Overview

Prayer and worship are closely connected. In this session we will examine a way to reach out to God in prayer with grateful hearts. We will explore an ancient Hebrew form of prayer called the *berakah,* which captures both our desire to praise God and our need for God in our lives. We will learn to write and pray our own *berakahs.*

If you are using this guide on your own, you may omit the section entitled "Open."

To begin, pray the following *berakah* aloud (in unison with your group if you have a group):

Blessed art Thou, O God, creator of the universe and Father of all creation. Grant to us this day the ability to praise you in ways that express our love for you and our desire to live as sons and daughters in your holy family. Amen.

OPEN   20-30 MINUTES

Giving Thanks

Even when life is tough, there are those moments when we feel a sense of gratitude. What triggers thankfulness in you?

1. Did you "say grace" at mealtime when you were a kid? If so, how did you feel about that? If not, what did you think of those who do?

2. What are the occasions at which you feel most thankful?

❏ Thanksgiving   ❏ getting out of bed each day
❏ weddings   ❏ mealtime
❏ when praying   ❏ when success strikes
❏ holidays in general   ❏ when summer comes
❏ concerts   ❏ in church
❏ in relationships   ❏ other:

3. Pick one thing for which you are grateful today and share it with the group.

THE NATURE OF BLESSING   5 MINUTES

The Bible is filled with blessings. Kings pronounce blessings on their subjects (2 Samuel 19:39); families bless their children (Genesis 24:60, 27:1-40). But mostly, everybody blesses God.

For example, in Genesis 24 Abraham sends his servant back to his clan to find a wife for his son Isaac. When the servant arrives in Nahor, he stops at the local well. There he prays, asking God that the right young woman would offer him and his camels water to drink. Even before he finishes praying, Rebekah appears and offers him water and a room with her family for the night. Instead of thanking God (or Rebekah), the servant blesses God: "Blessed be the LORD, the God of my master Abraham, who has not forsaken his steadfast love and his faithfulness toward my master" (Genesis 24:27, NRSV). Later, when he tells this story to Rebekah's brother and father and they agree that Rebekah can marry Isaac, he again blesses God (verse 48).

When Israelites blessed God, they were acknowledging who God is. They were declaring the character of God. To bless God is to praise God. It is "speaking well about God."

Blessing God became a daily habit for the Israelites. At meals a *berakah* (a blessing) was pronounced (Deuteronomy 8:10). The *berakah* began with the words, "Blessed are you, Lord God, ruler of the universe," and was completed by a statement that proclaimed God's deeds. For example, "Blessed are you, Lord God, ruler of the universe who created the fruit of the vine," or "Blessed are you, Lord God, ruler of the universe who feeds the whole earth with his good things."[1] Jesus offered a *berakah* at the Last Supper, and it became the basis of the prayer that churches still uses at communion (Matthew 26:26-27; 1 Corinthians 10:16, 11:23-26). Perhaps the most comprehensive prayer of blessing in the New Testament is in Ephesians 1. The whole chapter is a single prayer that begins, "Blessed be the God and Father of our Lord" (Ephesians 1:3, NRSV).

Here are some other prayers of blessing found in the Bible:

❖ Blessed be the LORD, the God of Israel, who alone does wondrous things. Blessed be his glorious name forever; may his glory fill the whole earth. Amen and Amen. (Psalm 72:18-19, NRSV)

❖ Blessed be the LORD, who has delivered you from the Egyptians and from Pharaoh. (Exodus 18:10, NRSV)

❖ Blessed be the LORD, who has given rest to his people Israel according to all that he promised; not one word has failed of all that he promised, which he spoke through his servant Moses. The LORD our God be with us, as he was with our ancestors; may he not leave us or abandon us, but incline our hearts to him, to walk in all his ways, and to keep his commandments, his statutes, and his ordinances, which he commanded our ancestors. Let these words of mine with which I pleaded before the LORD, be near to the LORD our God day and night, and may he maintain the cause of his servant and the cause of his people Israel, as each day requires; so that all the people of the earth may know that the Lord is God; there is no other. (1 Kings 8:56-60, NRSV)

27

PRAYER EXERCISE[2]   **20-30 MINUTES**

Notice the composition of the prayers of blessing listed above.

- ❖ They all begin with the phrase, "Blessed be the LORD."
- ❖ They then add a statement about God: who he is or what he has done.
- ❖ They sometimes end with a request (see the final example).

4. Discuss the long *berakah* from 1 Kings 8.

   a. What attributes or actions of God are named in this prayer?

   b. What requests are made of him?

   c. What is the underlying attitude toward God as seen in this prayer?

5. Write your own *berakah*.

   a. Think through which characteristic or action of God you want to praise him for.

   b. What request do you want to make of God? Let your request flow as a natural consequence of who you have declared God to be. For example: "Blessed be the Lord who in his healing power mends and binds our wounds and brokenness. Grant to your servant _____, the experience of your healing power as he deals with his illness."

   c. Do not be afraid to write two or three *berakahs*. Ask God to lead you.

6. Pray your *berakah* aloud. If you are meeting with a group, divide into sub-groups of about four people. One person begins by praying aloud his or her prayer of blessing. After this prayer of blessing, others may join in with praise to God focused on the attribute and request of the *berakah*. Repeat the same process until each person has prayed his or her *berakah*.

7. Discuss this prayer experience.

   a. What was the experience of writing a *berakah* like for you?

   b. How might you use this type of prayer on your own? With groups?

BLESS YOU   **10-20 MINUTES**

One of the best gifts a parent can give a child when he or she comes of age is a blessing. A blessing is a form of affirmation. It says yes to that child: "Yes, you are now an adult. Yes, you are precious and wonderful. Yes, you matter, you count, you can make your way successfully into the life that extends before you." However, not all children are so blessed. Some parents are unable or unwilling to give such a blessing. Others are just unaware of the need to bless. We get our blessings from a variety of places. How have you been "blessed"?

8. Who is the person (if anyone) who has pronounced a blessing on you?

❏ a parent	❏ a teacher
❏ a spouse	❏ a grandparent
❏ a minister	❏ a relative
❏ a friend	❏ a group
❏ no one	❏ other:

9. In what ways has this blessing empowered you? Or, how has a lack of blessing handicapped you?

10. In whose life can you appropriately pronounce a blessing?

Consider the following three blessings found in the Gospels:

❖ At Jesus' baptism, God the Father says, "You are my Son, whom I love; with you I am well pleased." (Mark 1:11)

❖ In the story of the prodigal child, the father says to his son, "Let's have a feast and celebrate. For this son of mine was dead and is alive again; he was lost and is found.'" (Luke 15:23-24)

❖ In the story of the prodigal child, the father says to the older brother: "My son, you are always with me, and everything I have is yours." (Luke 15:31)

11. With which of these blessings do you resonate? Spend time
in silent prayer receiving this blessing from God. Open
yourself to God. Let God bless you.

12. In any time you have remaining, discuss this experience of
blessing.

CLOSING PRAYER   5 MINUTES

End by praying the following prayer of blessing, which was
composed in the thirteenth century by St. Francis of Assisi.
(Pray in unison if you are meeting with a group.)

> *You are holy, Lord, the only God,*
> *and your deeds are wonderful.*
> *You are strong.*
> *You are great.*
> *You are the Most High, you are almighty.*
> *You, holy Father, are King of heaven and earth.*
> *You are Three and One,*
> *Lord God, all good.*
> *You are Good, all Good, supreme Good,*
> *Lord God, living and true.*
> *You are love,*
> *You are wisdom.*
> *You are humility, you are endurance.*
> *You are rest, you are peace.*
> *You are joy and gladness.*
> *You are justice and moderation.*
> *You are all our riches, And you suffice for us.*
> *You are beauty.*
> *You are gentleness.*
> *You are our protector, you are our guardian and defender.*
> *You are courage.*
> *You are our haven and our hope.*
> *You are our faith,*
> *Our great consolation.*
> *You are our eternal life, Great and wonderful Lord,*
> *God almighty, Merciful Saviour.*[3]

REFLECTION
Adoration

Adoration lies at the heart of praise and worship. Richard Foster defines adoration as "the spontaneous yearning of the heart to worship, honor, magnify, and bless God."[4] The word "spontaneous" may trouble us. What if we don't feel in a praiseful mood? Sure, there are those times when our hearts are filled with gratitude to God, when we are overwhelmed by his love, power, or presence. At such moments it is hard *not* to praise God. But these are the exception, not the rule. For most of us, life is difficult, and when we cry out to God it is more apt to be "Help" than "Thanks."

On the other hand, with a little thought most of us *can* find things for which to praise God. Just asking the question, "For what are you thankful to God?" triggers our memory. We recall all the general blessings of life: air to breath, good health, a place to stay, food, friends, family, church. As we make a list of such blessings, it grows quickly. Because most of the blessings we name are assumed parts of life, we do not notice them unless we are asked or we are deprived of them. How wonderful are all the blessings that surround us like air and sunshine! But beyond the general blessings shared by most people, we remember particular blessings: a calling, a job we love, a creative challenge, a special friend.

In this (and following) sessions, we will encounter a series of words that are used interchangeably: *praise, thanksgiving, worship, blessing, adoration, honor,* and *exultation.* Each has its own definition but they all circle around the same issue: how we respond to a God who loves us so inordinately. Each word touches on an aspect of how we express our deeply felt gratitude to God. Perhaps we should not try to separate too carefully the different words. Perhaps we need to let them simply remain meshed together, accessing individual emphases as need demands, knowing that we are getting at the core of prayer as response to God.

In the end, adoration is noticing. It is lingering over that which speaks of God: a lily, a kind word, a passage from Scripture, a sense of peace. In the lingering is the awareness that this is of God. Adoration is the easy gratitude that follows

reflexively from such an insight. When we do not win the battle
of time, we find it difficult to praise God. We are too busy to
stop, notice, and respond to God in that noticing.

WEEKLY EXERCISES

Each day: Begin your prayer time with a *berakah*. Do this by
considering the attributes of God listed for the day. Reflect on
this facet of God and remember the ways in which you have
experienced this reality. Then compose your *berakah* for the
day, beginning with the phrase, "Blessed be the LORD," and then
adding (1) a statement about this particular attribute of God
and (2) a request related to the attribute. Pray this *berakah* over
and over for the day until it is part of you and your conversation with God.

For example, if you focus on the statement, "God is love,"
then you might compose the following *berakahs*:

> *"Blessed be the LORD who in his creative love made this earth
> and all the creatures in it. May your love be revealed today
> throughout your creation and especially in my own heart as I
> seek to love your creation and the people you have created.
> Amen."*

> *"Blessed be the LORD who is Love itself. Grant that I might live
> in your house of Love, today and all days. Amen."*

You may want to write several *berakahs* for each theme. As
you write, don't try too hard. Just let the words flow. Let God
give you the prayer you are to pray. Share your *berakahs* with
several others.

Day one: God is love. In what ways do you know this God who
is said to be love itself? See 1 John 4:7-12.

Day two: God is longsuffering. How have you known God's
patience? See Psalm 86:15-16 and Colossians 3:12.

Day three: God is tender. In what ways have you experienced
God's tenderness? See Isaiah 40:11 and Psalm 103:13-14.

Day four: God is powerful. In what ways have you experienced God's incomparable power? See Isaiah 40:10-29.

Day five: God is seeking. In what ways have you experienced the fact that God knows you and seeks you even when you are hiding? See Isaiah 41:8-10.

Notes

1. Thomas Worden, *The Psalms Are Christian Prayer* (London: Geoffrey Chapman, 1964), p. 69.
2. It was Professor Dean Borgman who first pointed out to me the use of the *berakah* in the Old Testament and did an exercise with my students in which they wrote out their own prayers of blessing.
3. This is recorded in *The Oxford Book of Prayer*, edited by George Appleton (London: Oxford University Press, 1985), pp. 62-63.
4. *The Oxford Book of Prayer*, p. 81.

Prayer of Worship

Psalm 100

Group Note:
Leader's Notes for this session can be found on page 107.

Overview

Prayer and worship are closely linked. The Psalms have long been a prime vehicle for worship, as well as the church's guidebook to prayer. In this session we will examine a psalm of praise—Psalm 100—and use it to learn how to praise and worship God.

To begin, pray Psalm 100 aloud (see pages 36-37). If you are meeting with a group, pray the psalm responsively. That is, the leader will read the first verse, the rest of the group will respond with the second verse; the leader will read the third verse; and so on until the final verse is read together. In the atmosphere of prayer, ask God's blessing on today's session. Ask for the grace to worship God with full and grateful hearts.

OPEN   20-30 MINUTES
Covenant
Every group needs ground rules by which it operates. A suggested set of small group guidelines is found on page 10. Use the "Open" exercise today to discuss your group covenant. Can you give yourself to this covenant for the time period during which the group meets?

1. Examine together the group covenant on page 10. Are there any guidelines that you think need to be deleted or altered?

2. Are there other guidelines that you think might profitably be added?

3. In the time that you have already met together, what is one thing you have come to value about this group?

TEXT   5 MINUTES
"Most Christians for most of the Christian centuries have learned to pray by praying the Psalms." This is how Eugene Peterson begins the introduction to his new paraphrase of the Psalms.[1] It makes sense, then, for us to allow the Psalms to tutor us in prayer.

Psalm 100 is a psalm of praise. It is simple, honest, brimming with joy, and unambiguous in its thankfulness. It is a good place to learn how to worship God because worship is its sole focus.

Psalm 100 has been widely used in the church. In the Episcopal *Book of Common Prayer* it is known as *Jubilate Deo* ("O be joyful to God"). Two well-known hymns use its words (paraphrased): William Kethe's "All people that on earth do dwell" and Isaac Watt's "Before Jehovah's awful throne."

[1]Shout for joy to the LORD, all the earth.
[2]Worship the LORD with gladness;
come before him with joyful songs.

36

³Know that the LORD is God.
    It is he who made us, and we are his;
    we are his people, the sheep of his pasture.
⁴Enter his gates with thanksgiving
    and his courts with praise;
    give thanks to him and praise his name.
⁵For the LORD is good and his love endures forever;
    his faithfulness continues through all generations.
(Psalm 100)

ANALYSIS   **10-15 MINUTES**

4. List the seven commands that form the essence of this
   psalm.

    Verse 1:

    Verse 2a:

    Verse 2b:

    Verse 3:

    Verse 4a:

    Verse 4b:

    Verse 4c:

5. What spiritual activity do these verbs describe?

6. What three qualities of God are the basis for this exuberant
   worship (verse 5)? What does each term tell us about the
   nature and character of this God (as opposed to other
   gods)?

APPLICATION   **15-30 MINUTES**

7. a. Based on the components of worship named in Psalm 100, how would you define the act of worship?

   b. How does your definition compare to your experience of worship?

   c. What aspect of worship do you need to work on?

8. a. How have you experienced the goodness of God? The love of God? The faithfulness of God?

   b. In what ways is all this the basis for your worship of God?

9. What does it mean to pray to this sort of God? For example, what would prayer be like if God were evil (not good), filled with hate (not love), and unreliable (not faithful)? Remember that this negative conception of God can be found in the cultural understanding of various peoples in history.

10. What have you learned about the connection between prayer and worship? How can the Psalms be used in your prayer and worship?

CLOSING PRAYER   10 MINUTES

End this session with a time of free prayer in thanks, praise, and worship of God. Make God the focus of these prayers, remembering who God is and what his gifts to you are. Close by praying Psalm 150, which is another great hymn of praise.

If you are meeting with a group, give everyone a chance to join in the free prayer with prayers of a sentence or two. Then pray Psalm 150 in unison.

> Praise the LORD.
> Praise God in his sanctuary;
>   praise him in his mighty heavens.
> Praise him for his acts of power;
>   praise him for his surpassing greatness.
> Praise him with the sounding of the trumpet,
>   praise him with the harp and lyre,
> praise him with tambourine and dancing,
>   praise him with the strings and flute,
> praise him with the clash of cymbals,
>   praise him with resounding cymbals.
> Let everything that has breath praise the LORD.
> Praise the LORD. (Psalm 150)

WEEKLY EXERCISES

Reflect on the worship of God. *Each day:* Focus on one of the seven attributes of worship given in Psalm 100. (You might wish to discuss the daily questions with a friend, or write your responses in your journal.) Begin and end each day's prayer with one of the other seven psalms in this collection of psalms of praise (Psalms 93-99).[2]

Day one: Focus on what it means to worship God with shouts of joy. What kind of exuberance can you bring to God? What is it about God that brings joy to you? Worship God in this way. Use Psalm 93 in your prayer.

Day two: Focus on what it means to serve God with gladness. In what ways is worship service? In what ways is service worship? What is your service to God? How do you worship God? Worship God in this way. Use Psalm 94 in your prayer.

Day three: Focus on what it means to come before God with songs. What songs (or type of music) facilitate your worship of God? How can you incorporate song into your prayers? Is there one song you can begin to use in your worship? Worship God in this way. Use Psalm 95 in your prayer.

Day four: Focus on what it means to acknowledge who God is because you know God's character, deeds, and relationship to you. Worship God in this way. Use Psalm 96 in your prayer.

Day five: Focus on what it means to come before God in his holy place. What places and spaces are sacred to you? Where do you meet God? Worship God in this way. Use Psalm 97 in your prayer.

Day six: Focus on what it means to give God thanks. Make a list of all the things, general and specific, for which you thank God. Let this list then be the basis of your prayer today. Worship God in this way. Use Psalm 98 in your prayer.

Day seven: Focus on what it means to give God praise. In terms of your life during the past twenty-four hours, what do you want to praise God for? Worship God in this way. Use Psalm 99 in your prayer.

BACKGROUND NOTES

Setting: Psalm 100 is the final in a series of eight psalms that praise God. They were probably composed for a great religious festival in which the kingship of God was lauded, and they were probably meant to be sung.

The seven imperative verbs in the first four verses of Psalm 100 are an extended call to worship. Verse 5 explains why such worship is fitting: because of who God is (good, loving, faithful).

Hebrew poetry works through parallelism rather than rhyme. An idea is expressed in one line only to be re-expressed in the next line to amplify the idea. Notice this in Psalm 100.

Verse 1: When the psalmist calls us to "shout for joy," he has in mind a royal fanfare offered to a worthy king. (Compare Psalm 98:4-6.) The whole earth is called upon to join in this acclamation because God is the God of the whole planet.

At the heart of worship is a shout of joy. Worship is not meant to be a solemn obligation undertaken to appease a terrifying God. Judeo-Christian worship springs from profound gratitude to a good and loving God. Notice how often joy and gladness appear in this psalm.

Verse 2: The verb translated "worship" also can be translated "serve." To worship is to serve God; it is to live as his joyful follower; it is to do that which brings praise to his name. The word translated "joyful songs" implies exuberant singing.

Understanding worship as service and service as worship means that we are no longer restricted to Sunday morning when it comes to worship: our active service of God is part of our worship.

Verse 3: To "know" is to recognize, confess, or acknowledge who God is: the LORD (Yahweh or Jehovah). God's name recalls the long history during which he chose Israel from all the peoples of the earth to reveal to the rest of the world who God is. The acknowledgment of Yahweh as God stems from knowledge of God's deeds—that God created us and that the peoples of the earth are God's family.

We can worship in this uninhibited fashion because we know who God is.

Verse 5: Three qualities of God are identified as the basis for the sevenfold worship of God: God is good, loving, and faithful. God is not evil (unlike some of the ancient gods). Rather, God is the source of all that makes life wonderful and worthwhile. Furthermore, this is an active good. God delivers us from evil and brings about that which gives life. The word translated "love" is a special Hebrew word that is hard to capture in English. It means "steadfast love," "loyal love," or "unfailing love." It refers to the kind of relationship that exists between God the loving parent and God's children, and to God's reliable care that endures forever. The word "faithful" stresses the reliability of God. God's faithfulness is linked to God's promises. God will act as God promised. The fact of God's faithfulness is the basis for much prayer in the Old Testament. The petitioner bases his or her prayer on the fact that God has promised to do thus and so and is faithful to perform.

Notes
1. *The Message: Psalms* (Colorado Springs, Colo.: NavPress, 1994), p. 5.
2. Please note that instead of the usual exercises for five days there are seven exercises because of the seven attributes in Psalm 100.

Meditative Prayer

ENTERING PRAYER THROUGH THE DOORWAY OF SCRIPTURE

Group Note:
Leader's Notes for this session can be found on page 108.

Overview
Meditation and prayer are closely connected. When we meditate on a passage from Scripture, we are drawn automatically into prayer—if we let ourselves be.
In this session we will explore the use of imagination in making a passage of Scripture into a place of prayer.

In your opening prayer, read Zechariah 2:10 aloud twice (if you are working on your own) or listen with your eyes closed as your leader reads it aloud twice (if you are meeting with a group). In your meditation listen for those words or phrases that resonate with you. Then pray aloud, offering to God what you have been feeling and thinking in your meditation on Zechariah 2:10.

> *"Shout and be glad, O Daughter of Zion. For I am coming, and I will live among you," declares the LORD.*

OPEN   **20-30 MINUTES**

Reflecting

You do it all the time but hardly notice: you reflect on the world around you. You read a striking story in the newspaper, then sit back and let it play over and over in your mind. A driver cuts you off and you start an inner litany on how discourteous drivers are. As you leave church with the final anthem still ringing in your ears, you muse upon what a mighty fortress God really is. *Harnessing the power of musing is a great way to pray.* How good are you at reflecting on your life?

1. In the following list, which experience is most likely to capture your attention and move you to reflection? Why?

   ❏ a piece of music   ❏ a newspaper article
   ❏ a sunset   ❏ a walk in the woods
   ❏ a passage of Scripture   ❏ a painful experience
   ❏ a conversation   ❏ a movie
   ❏ a letter from home   ❏ a painting
   ❏ a book   ❏ other:
   ❏ a television program

2. Are your musings mostly positive or mostly negative?

3. When you think about things, what are you apt to do?

   ❏ write it down   ❏ forget about it
   ❏ pray   ❏ puzzle over it for days
   ❏ write a song   ❏ I don't reflect much
   ❏ seek more information   ❏ other:
   ❏ tell a friend

THE PROCESS OF MEDITATIVE PRAYER   **10 MINUTES**

At the heart of meditative prayer is Scripture. In meditative prayer we enter into a story from the Bible by means of our imaginations, becoming one of the characters, watching the action unfold, speaking to Jesus, hearing Jesus speak to us. Learn the process by doing the following exercise.

Step one: Choose a story from the Bible. It is probably best to begin with an account from the Gospels when you are first learning this way of prayer. Gospel stories are familiar to many of us, they connect with our issues, and they are brief. As such, they are easy to grasp and easy to imagine.

Step two: Read the story several times. As you do so, pay attention to the details of the passage. Notice the setting, the characters, and the situation. Who is the central figure? What is the problem? What is the outcome? What is unusual about this story? How does it connect with your life situation? Read the account enough times to understand its main point and be familiar with its details.

Step three: Get quiet in yourself and focus on openness to God. Find a place and a posture that will allow you to meditate. Relax your body. Slow your breathing. At the same time be in prayer, asking God for guidance. You may want to use a centering prayer as a way of focusing your mind and quieting the inner noises.

Step four: Imagine yourself as a participant in the story. You may be an on-looker or you may be involved in the action, but put yourself in that place and time. Begin by noticing the details in the story. What do you see? Smell? Feel? Hear? Taste? Think? Watch the situation as it unfolds. Listen to what is said. What is said to you? If Jesus is in the story, go to him. Tell him about your concerns. Listen to his response. Reply to him.

Step five: Let your mind move slowly from the past to the present. Take with you the "feel" of the whole experience. Present that to God. Be open to God. Thank God. Listen to God.

Step six: Record the experience. If you have a journal, describe the experience. If you are in the group, share your experience. Be open to new insights as you journal or as you recount your experience.

PRAYER EXERCISE   20-30 MINUTES

Step one: The Passage
The passage you will use is taken from Luke's account of the birth of Jesus. An angel appears to a group of shepherds to announce the birth and what it means. Begin by examining the story briefly to get it firmly in mind.

> ⁸And there were shepherds living out in the fields nearby, keeping watch over their flocks at night. ⁹An angel of the Lord appeared to them, and the glory of the Lord shone around them, and they were terrified. ¹⁰But the angel said to them, "Do not be afraid. I bring you good news of great joy that will be for all the people. ¹¹Today in the town of David a Savior has been born to you; he is Christ the Lord. ¹²This will be a sign to you: You will find a baby wrapped in cloths and lying in a manger."
>
> ¹³Suddenly a great company of the heavenly host appeared with the angel, praising God and saying, ¹⁴"Glory to God in the highest, and on earth peace to men on whom his favor rests." (Luke 2:8-14)

Step two: Discuss the Story
  ❖ What is the setting? Where does it take place? When?
  ❖ What do you know about shepherds?
  ❖ What does this account tell you about the angel? The heavenly hosts?
  ❖ What is their message? Who is this baby?
  ❖ How do the shepherds respond to the angel? What do you imagine they were thinking and feeling when the heavenly company departed?

Step three: Centering
Prepare yourself for prayer.

  ❖ Sit comfortably with eyes closed.
  ❖ Relax your body and slow your breathing.
  ❖ Open yourself to God. You might wish to pray a breath prayer to focus your heart.

Step four: Imaginative Prayer

If you are working on your own, read the passage one more
time. If you are meeting with a group, let the leader read the
story while you close your eyes. Imagine yourself there with
the shepherds. Take about five minutes for silent meditation
and conversation with God. (If you are on your own, you can
set a timer. If you are with a group, the leader will call you
back to the present at the end of the meditation.)

Step five: Discussion

Talk or journal about this experience.

- ❖ Describe briefly your experience.
- ❖ Was this easy or difficult for you?
- ❖ In what ways were you with God while praying this way?

UNDERSTANDING MEDITATIVE PRAYER   15 MINUTES

If you only have one hour for your small group, skip this section and go straight to "Closing Prayer." Assign this section as homework. If you have time, take a few minutes to discuss meditative prayer based on the following comments:

❖ Different people have different abilities when it comes to the use of the imagination. For some, the use of imagination is a snap. They see the setting with clarity; they hear the words being spoken; they can enter into the conversation. They can touch the angel and feel the pulsing glory of God. They even hear the heavenly hosts singing with haunting beauty the song of praise to God. But other people struggle. When asked to "imagine the following scene," they see little or nothing—or what they imagine is quite different from what they think they should be seeing. Whatever your experience in doing meditative prayer, accept it, don't fight it. We each have our own styles of prayer best suited to us (as we will discuss in session eight). It has been said that about 15 percent of any group of people simply cannot get their imaginations to work in this way.

❖ In this kind of prayer, we do not do anything; we just let prayer happen. This can be frustrating if you view prayer as something you have to do, like asking God for certain things, praising God, or saying certain prayers. In meditative prayer what we "do" is open ourselves to God by imagining that we are part of a biblical story. This then becomes the place or space in which we are available to God. As we so meditate, what happens is up to God. For some people this can be the first step in moving from prayer as doing to prayer as being.

❖ Once you have let yourself imagine a situation like the coming of the angel to the shepherds, you can easily return again and again to that situation. You can let the dialogue continue as you grow more familiar with the situation. It can become a sacred place for you.

❖ Meditative prayer is similar is some ways to *lectio divina*, the process of sacred reading. In *lectio divina*, Scripture is read slowly, aloud, until a word or phrase strikes you. Then you mull over that word or phrase until it becomes a prayer to God. *Lectio divina* is discussed in another study guide in this series, *Contemplative Bible Reading*.

❖ The words meditation and contemplation often are used interchangeably. However, they also can be used to describe quite different processes. Meditation involves filling our minds with images. Contemplation involves emptying our minds of images. In meditation we respond to God out of what we see and hear and feel. In contemplation, we rest silently in the presence of God. This is the difference between active and passive prayer: reaching out to God versus waiting for God.[1] Meditation is an art that most Christians can master. Contemplation is for those who are experienced in the things of the Spirit.

CLOSING PRAYER   5 MINUTES

Commit your experiences of meditative prayer to God and ask him to teach you how to pray in such a way that touches his presence. End by praying a prayer from Julian of Norwich (1342-1443):

> *God, of your goodness give me yourself for you are sufficient for me. I cannot properly ask anything less, to be worthy of you. If I were to ask less, I should always be in want. In you alone do I have all.*[2]

HOMEWORK

In the next session you will work with the prayer of *examen*. There is a longer than usual explanation of this particular prayer style. If you are meeting with a group, it will speed up the next meeting if you read those pages before coming to the group.

REFLECTION

The Return: A Meditation on the Story of the Prodigal Son
Here is how the story of the prodigal son might unfold in your
imagination with you as a participant. The story is picked up at
the point when the prodigal "comes to his senses" and decides
to return home. You are his companion, who returns home
with him. Read over the original account in Luke 15:11-32 so
you have the story clearly in mind. Focus on verses 15-24. As
you read the meditation that follows, fill in the details from
your own life at those points marked "Add your own reflections." Read this meditation in an atmosphere of prayer.
Imagine that you are there, telling this story.

*It was the hunger that finally got to us—the feeling that comes
when you have not had any real food for days on end. Our stom-
achs were groaning with the pain of the knots inside. It got so bad
that all we could think of was food. The horizon of our interest had
reduced to one issue and one issue only: eating.*

*"I can't stand this anymore" my companion cried out one day
in his misery. We had just returned from feeding the pigs. Imagine
us, Jews, feeding pigs. We were that low. Once again we had
stolen a few, miserable bites from their slop. This would be all we
got to eat.*

*"At my father's farm," said my friend, "even the hired hands
have plenty to eat. If only I were home." I, too, thought of how I
had gotten to this place. I remembered my bad choices, my willful-
ness, pride, disdain. . . . (Add your own reflections.)*

*"I'm going home," he announced. "I've had it. I'll get a job on
my father's farm. I'll become a hired hand. To think I once owned a
part of that great farm!"*

*The trek back to his home was hard beyond belief. We stole
what little food we ate. Some people were kind to us along the way,
but mostly they saw us for who we had become—down-on-our-
luck bums, drunks, disheveled, shuffling along to God-knows-
where. My friend was preoccupied most of the time, but I knew
what he was doing: composing his speech to his father. He kept trying out words and phrases on me. What struck me was his honesty.
No more pretense. No more denial. Just the bitter truth. He had
given up being a son, and now he was the lowest of the low. No*

*one's fault but his own. He had no rights, no expectations. He could
only hope for common mercy. Maybe his father would give him a
job. Maybe not. He would not blame his father if he simply turned
his back on him. As he went on composing, I worked on my
speech—if I ever went home. . . . (Add your own reflections.)*

    *I will never forget my first glimpse of the farm. It was even
more beautiful than my friend had described: the gentle hills, the
endless fields ripe with grain and vegetables, the orchards with their
fruit. The day was beautiful, too, with sun flashing gold everywhere
and a soft breeze that carried indescribable aromas. The farm was
so lovely in its proportions, with trees in all the right places and a
stream that ran through it creating pools. There was an overwhelm-
ing atmosphere of peace. . . . (Add your own reflections.)*

    *Then my friend spotted his father—a lone figure in the dis-
tance. He saw us. We could see him straining to identify who we
were. He couldn't look away, as if he knew who we were—or at
least hoped that we were who he wanted to see.*

    *Then he was sure. He cast his staff to the side and ran, actually
ran, to greet us. Of course, it was his son who was the focus of his
attention. But even then I felt included in what was happening. My
friend could not believe his eyes. He dropped to his knees, head down.
Then his father was upon us, literally. He dragged my friend to his
feet and embraced him as passionately as I have ever seen a father
hug and kiss a son. In fact, it was unlike any embrace I had seen
before. It contained joy and pain and love and suffering, plus a dozen
other emotions I could not read. . . . (Add your own reflections.)*

    *My friend launched into his confession speech, but it was as if
the father did not even hear it. "Bring fresh clothes," he cried to his
servants, who had flocked out of the house. "Prepare a feast, a ban-
quet. We will celebrate as we have never celebrated before." Then
he said words I will never forget; words that were directed to his
son but included me, as if this were my home and he was also my
father: "This son of mine was dead and is alive again; he was lost
and is found." (Hear your Heavenly Father say these words to you.
Let him embrace you and welcome you home.)*

WEEKLY EXERCISES

Each day: Pray meditatively during this week. Listed below are passages you may wish to use. In each of these, Jesus is involved in conflict of some sort. We are challenged to hear in the voices of the others our own fears, assumptions, misunderstandings, and needs.

You may find one passage that you want to stick with for part of the week or all week because it resonates deeply with you and you realize there is still meaning to be gained from it.

Day one: Love. Read Mark 14:3-9. This is the story of the woman who anointed Jesus with expensive perfume, preparing him for his coming death. (At that time, bodies were commonly anointed before burial.) Notice the strong emotions.

Day two: Kingdom. Read Mark 10:13-16. Again there is tension between Jesus and his disciples. Their reactions often are our reactions if we were able to express them. Jesus reveals the key to being a part of his kingdom.

Day three: Possessions. Read Mark 10:17-27. The story of the rich young ruler challenges us to re-evaluate our view of possessions and our view of morality.

Day four: Religion. Read Mark 11:15-18. Jesus cleanses the temple of those merchants who are taking advantage of the religious obligations of the poor. In so doing, he becomes a model for us of righteous indignation and challenges us to be honorable in our role in the community.

Day five: Service. Read Mark 10:35-45. In defining his role as Messiah as that of a suffering servant who gives his life for others, Jesus defines how his followers are to relate to others.

Notes

1. Technically, this is the difference between cataphatic and apophatic ways of spirituality: spirituality that makes use of images and other sensory data, and spirituality that feels God is so beyond human comprehension that to use images is to distort God (all we can do is wait in a "cloud of unknowing").
2. *The Oxford Book of Prayer*, p. 66.

Prayer of *Examen*

PROCESSING YOUR DAY
BEFORE GOD

Group Note:
Leader's Notes for
this session can be
found on page 109

Overview

The prayer of *examen* comes to us from
the sixteenth century and enables us to
process each day before God. The three-
step process begins with *gratitude*, moves
to *awareness of God's presence*, and ends with *confession*. In this
session you will examine the details of the process, pray a prayer
of *examen*, and then discuss or journal the experience.

In the silence of reflection, recall the past twenty-four hours
and locate one or two experiences, feelings, or encounters for
which you are grateful to God. As you do so, name them aloud
by saying, "Thank you Lord for. . . ." (If you are with a group,
allow everyone a chance to pray.) Conclude by praying aloud
this prayer of thanksgiving.

*We (I) thank you, O God, for your great and wonderful bless-
ings given to us so freely. We thank you for the world in which
we live, for the tasks you have given us to perform, and especially for the people with whom you have surrounded us. Give
us eyes to see your manifold blessings and hearts to rejoice in
these great gifts. We pray in the name of Jesus Christ who is
himself your greatest gift to us. Amen.*

OPEN   **20-30 MINUTES**

Recollection

Memory is an art to be developed. Without it, life just passes us by. How good are you at remembering?

1. Briefly share one positive memory from each of these periods in your life:

   a. Early childhood

   b. Teenage years

   c. First job

2. What recollection tools do you use?

   ❑ a diary
   ❑ a journal
   ❑ thinking about things a lot
   ❑ telling the story to others
   ❑ I don't forget
   ❑ I forget everything anyway
   ❑ my spouse remembers
   ❑ letters to friends
   ❑ making family stories
   ❑ other:

3. Who has the best memory in your family? Why?

THE PRAYER OF *EXAMEN*   15 MINUTES

The word *examen* has a strange but familiar ring to it. It feels
like an English word but not really. It sounds like *examination*,
but not quite. In fact, it comes from the Latin and is related to
the concept of examination. But the word actually describes the
indicator on a scale that points to the true weight of something
placed on that scale. It means an accurate assessment of a situation. The prayer of *examen* is *a way of assessing one's life before
God on a regular basis.* This way to pray was first developed by
St. Ignatius, the founder of the Society of Jesus. He urged all
the members of his society to use this prayer daily, even when
the necessities of travel, work, and ministry made other forms
of prayer impossible.

Recollection is at the root of the prayer of *examen.* The Bible
is filled with calls to remember: Remember how God called
Abraham and made a covenant with him. Remember how God
rescued his people from Egypt. Remember the Law that God
gave his people. Remember in the bread and wine the Savior
who died for your sins. Our history, both as individuals and as
members of a community, is a key ingredient in our prayer. It is
the context within which we approach God.

The prayer of *examen* asks us to focus our recollection on a
narrow time span: the previous twenty-four hours. This seems
easy until we encounter the fact that most of our days go by
unnoticed. They just happen, and we are in bed before we
know it. We tend to glide through a day almost by rote unless
something stops us and makes us notice. The prayer of *examen*
is one way to prevent days from going by unexamined and
unlived.

Gratitude is the first step in the prayer of *examen.* We scan
the previous day looking for those events, experiences, ideas,
encounters, and conversations that came as good gifts to us and
that provoked (or should have provoked) gratitude. As we
recall the previous twenty-four hours we keep stopping and
saying, "O, yes, I remember. Thank you, Lord." No matter how
hard and troubling a day may have been, there are always
moments of grace if we have eyes to see them. It may be nothing more than, "Thank you, Lord, for air to breath and food to
eat." This is an acknowledgment that even in the midst of

struggle God continues his sustaining work in our lives. Regular practice of the prayer of *examen* can make us into grateful people, and this sense of gratitude helps us greatly.

Awareness of God is the second step in the prayer of *examen*. We go back over the same twenty-four hour period, this time looking for signs of God's presence. Sometimes these are easy to see: we recall the feeling of joy as we watched a pair of hawks soar high above and we knew that we too were made to soar; we read a psalm and there was a deep response in us that said, "Yes, this is what is true about the universe"; we had lunch with a friend and offered words of comfort that surprised even us and gave him hope. At other times God is hard to find. The sky is gray and empty; our heart is heavy; our mind is dull. But even then we know God is there: in our discontent we find seeds of new life; we also know that the sheer fact we are functioning as a human being is a gift of God's grace even though we cannot apprehend it. The prayer of *examen* can make us into the kind of person who lives constantly with the awareness of God. As such the very texture of how we live changes because the spiritual is not distant and remote but present and sustaining.[1]

Confession of failure is the final step in the prayer of *examen*. We recall again the previous twenty-four hours, except now we are alert to those times when we failed to live up to God's calling, when we chose against the way of love, when we passed by and refused to get involved. We search for those times when we refused the work of the Holy Spirit in our life, when we did not allow the Spirit to work in and through us. As we find these "refusals," we hold them up to the Lord in confession and repentance. We ask for forgiveness. In this atmosphere of gratitude and presence, confession feels different from when it emerges out of a sense of judgment. We have far less tendency to deny and avoid issues of failure and transgression when they come in the context of God's presence and work in our lives.

Here is an illustration of how the three-step process works:

> A beginner praying the *examen* may find it helpful to take one gift of the Spirit, for example, joy. He sees where he noticed joy in his day, and gives thanks; the places he

56

entered into the joy of another or allowed another to enter into his joy; the times joy was shared. These were the concrete moments when God was acting and working in his gift of joy for the person and in the others in his day. Conversely, he becomes aware of the times and places when he prevented God from acting for him in his gift of joy, when he would not enter into the joy of another, or when he was a kill-joy. The person sees this now and expresses his sorrow.[2]

In the end, the prayer of *examen* is about noticing: noticing the good gifts God gives us, noticing the presence of God in our lives, and noticing the ways we fail God. When we notice, we become more conscious. When we become more conscious, we grow.

PRAYER EXERCISE   20-30 MINUTES

The first half of the exercise will be done on your own (during your group meeting, if you are meeting with a group). Follow the instructions below and spend fifteen minutes working on and praying the prayer of *examen*. You may find it useful to have pen and paper.

❖ *Preparation*: Make a rough list of your activities for the previous day up to the present time, beginning with where you were at this time twenty-four hours ago (for instance, 8:00-10:00 P.M.: watched television; 10:00 P.M.-6:00 A.M.: sleep; 6:00-6:45 A.M.: got ready for work). This list will stimulate your memory of the previous day. Ask the Holy Spirit to enlighten you as you go back over this list looking for points of gratitude, the presence of God, and problems of obedience.

❖ *Step one*: Gratitude. Examine each time period to locate events, experiences, activities, encounters with people, and so on for which you are grateful to God. Thank God for each of these moments of grace.

❖ *Step two*: Awareness of God. Examine each time period for the presence of God. While it is true that God is present at each moment, you are seeking to notice those events, encounters, inner experiences, and activities in which the ever-present reality of God was especially real and apparent. Thank God for his presence.

❖ *Step three*: Confession. Review the previous twenty-four hours again. This time, look for those instances in which you failed to live up to your calling, in which you were a less-than-faithful disciple of Jesus by what you did or by what you failed to do. Ask God for forgiveness.

The second half of the exercise involves a discussion of your experience. Sharing and discussion after an experience of prayer will help you to grow in your understanding of the process by hearing from others. It is also a way to test what you are hearing from God. At times it is hard to know just what God is saying to us, but as we talk through our prayer with caring and sensitive others, we are able to grasp what God is calling us to.

If you are not meeting with a group, use these questions to help you reflect on your experience in your journal.

4. Describe your experience of doing the prayer of *examen.*

5. What did you learn from this experience?

   ❏ about this way of prayer?

   ❏ about yourself?

   ❏ about God's call?

CLOSING PRAYER   5 MINUTES

If you are meeting with a group, spend a few moments sharing the ways in which you have been aware of God's presence during this session. In prayer, thank and praise God for his presence. Ask for eyes to see God clearly. End by praying together a prayer written by Eric Milner-White (1884-1964).

> *Enter my heart, O Holy Spirit,*
> *come in blessed mercy and set me free.*
> *Throw open, O Lord, the locked doors of my mind;*
> *cleanse the chambers of my thought for thy dwelling:*
> *light these the fires of thine own holy brightness in new*
> *understandings of truth,*
> *O Holy Spirit, very God, whose presence is liberty,*
> *grant me the perfect freedom*
> *to be thy servant*
> *today, tomorrow, evermore. Amen.*[3]

REFLECTION
On Listening to God

Does God actually speak to us? We must face this question unless we are willing for prayer to be monologue only. Clearly, the men and women of the Bible thought God communicated with them. Abraham heard God tell him to leave his family home and journey to a new land where God said he would make a great nation of him (Genesis 12:1-3). Moses heard God speak at the burning bush (Exodus 3:4-14). Elijah heard the voice of God in the cave on Horeb (1 Kings 19:11-18). Job had an ongoing conversation with God, and prophets like Isaiah, Jeremiah, and Micah heard God and then spoke his word to others (Isaiah 6:8, 57:15; Jeremiah 1:4-7; Micah 6:8). At the time of Jesus' birth, Mary spoke with an angel sent from God, as did the shepherds and Zechariah (Luke 1:11-20,26-38; 2:8-15). Both Saul of Tarsus and Peter had visions in which God spoke (Acts 9:4-6, 10:13-15). And it is not only people of the Bible who have said God speaks to them. The same claim was made by Antony of Egypt (third century); Augustine (fifth century); Francis of Assisi and Thomas Aquinas (thirteenth century); Julian of Norwich (fourteenth century); Blaise Pascal (sixteenth century); Dag Hammarskjöld, Simone Weil, Frank Buchman, E. Stanley Jones, and Dallas Willard (twentieth century). This list could be extended enormously were it to include the testimonies of all the men and women down through the ages who have heard God.

It is one thing to assert that some people hear God; it is another to claim such a thing for oneself. Without a sense of presence, prayer becomes wishful thinking, pious reflection, or mechanical devotion. With a sense of presence, prayer becomes life-giving and wonderful. The problems of motivation and focus are dealt with. Nothing gets our attention nor our interest like a response from God. All lesser thoughts disappear like the wisps of vapor they are.

How does God speak? Various answers can be given: by inner impressions that have a sense of otherness to them ("a still, small voice"); through a passage from Scripture that resonates with us; via the intrusion of joy that has no obvious cause; through the voice of nature that sings the presence of its creator. But to hear, we have to notice and listen. We have to take the time for prayer to move from monologue to dialogue. It means stopping and waiting. "Be still and know that I am God" is how the psalmist puts it.

What does God's "voice" sound like? Certainly it is not audible and external like the words coming out of a radio (except in the most extraordinary circumstances). I would say God's voice has several characteristics. For one thing, it is spontaneous—it seems to come unbidden, not as the result of analysis. It is as if the constant inner dialogue that goes on in my mind is interrupted with an unexpected new note, gentle and kind. I suppose some hear God in demanding tones that brook no question, but for me, his voice is soft. It is also easily interrupted. I can intrude upon it, and I know when I am doing so.

Also, the insight I gain from hearing God is new. It does not have the sense of belonging to me. "I didn't know that" is often my response. "Where did that come from?" I am often surprised by the quality of the insight. In my experience that which seems to be divine insight consists mostly of spontaneous thoughts or ideas that appear in my mind when I am being consciously open to God.

Even as I write these words I hesitate. Who am I to claim this is God and not just my inner needs? Yet when I pay attention to such "impressions," there is a ring of truth about them. Yet the ever-present danger of misplaced attribution lurks in the background. Not all spontaneous thoughts, ideas, words, feelings, or visions are of God. Such impressions arise from many sources. In the end it seems to be a matter of *hesitant acceptance,* operating as if this is of God and then testing the insight against Scripture, the tradition of the Christian community, and common sense. Here is where the gift of discernment comes in. Spiritual direction is all about discernment: a director helping a directee to discern what God is saying. If the insight fits with what I know of God through these other sources, if it leads to wholeness and love, if it moves me forward in my spiritual perception, then I can live with this "intuition" as having the mark of God upon it. After all, we do walk by faith and not by sight.

What is the source of such divine impressions? I think they arise from the hidden center of our being, from our "heart," which is in constant touch with God, from where the Holy Spirit is at work uttering deep groanings that we do not apprehend. We seldom touch this true center of our beings, and when we do it is only obliquely and for an instant. But is not this the task of all ways of prayer: to put us in touch with that center so that what we pray is what is being prayed already?

WEEKLY EXERCISES

Each day: Take one fruit of the Spirit and use it as the grid through which you examine the previous twenty-four hours. For example, on Day one, review the day and find all the experiences of love that you have encountered. Give God thanks. Go back over these incidents a second time noticing God's presence and activity in each encounter. Finally, notice those times when you refused love, prevented love, or drew back from giving or receiving love. Ask God for forgiveness.

Day one: Love. Examine your life through the grid of love.

Day two: Joy. Examine your life through the grid of joy. Where did you encounter joy? How did God bring joy? How did you respond to joy?

Day three: Peace. Examine your life through the grid of peace. Where did you encounter peace? How did God bring peace? How did you respond to peace?

Day four: Goodness. Examine your life through the grid of goodness. Where did you encounter goodness? How did God bring goodness? How did you respond to goodness?

Day five: Self-Control. Examine your life through the grid of self-control. Where did you encounter self-control? How did God bring self-control? How did you respond to self-control?

Notes
1. See *Spiritual Autobiography* in this series, pages 89-103 ("The Discipline of Noticing") for seven ways in which we encounter God.
2. This is taken from an article, the title and source of which are unknown.
3. *The Oxford Book of Prayer*, p. 504.

Written Prayers

ENRICHING YOUR EXPERIENCE

Group Note:
Leader's Notes for this session can be found on page 110.

Overview
By now you have prayed a number of prayers written by other people, some from the Bible and some not. This may have been a new experience, because certain faith traditions stress spontaneous prayer rather than written prayer. Hopefully it has been a good experience for you. In this session you will explore the use of written prayers more directly. Your aim will be to enrich the quality of your prayer life and to expand your prayer vocabulary by exposing yourself to the wisdom and piety of men and women from across the ages.

Begin by praying a prayer of approach (or entrance to the service of worship) from the liturgy of St. John Chrysostom:

O God, our Master and our Lord, who hast appointed the heavenly orders and the hosts of angels and archangels for the service of thy glory: Grant that thy holy angels may enter with us as we enter, that they with us may serve thee and glorify thy goodness. Amen.[1]

OPEN   20-30 MINUTES
Church
Many of us learn to pray at church. Sometimes the lessons are
helpful, sometimes not. What has been your experience of
church?

1. Describe briefly your experience of church (if any) during
   each of the following time periods:

   a. Childhood

   b. Teenage years

   c. Currently

2. If you attend a church, what kind of prayer is offered there?

3. How significant is public prayer in your life?

WHY USE WRITTEN PRAYERS?   5 MINUTES
Some people don't like written prayers. They can become rote,
mere words that we rattle off without thinking or meaning.
And because connecting with God is an intensely personal
activity, how can others know our hearts and compose our
prayers? Those who grew up in a liturgical tradition in which
the prayers they read aloud as children never meant much to
them may be averse to using written prayers as adults.
   These are genuine problems. However, written prayers do

not have to be rote or disconnected from one's personal relationship with God. And the value of written prayers is substantial.

First, they connect us to the worldwide church down through the centuries. Prayers like the Lord's Prayer have been prayed by countless people, and we become a part of the company of saints who have reached out to God when we use them.

Second, printed prayers extend our prayer vocabularies. All of us get into a rut with our prayers. We tend to ask the same things in the same way over and over again. By means of the rich and powerful prayers of others we speak to God in ever-broader ways. Then in our spontaneous prayers we have a richer set of words and images to use in addressing God.

Third, there is good biblical precedence for the use of liturgical prayers. The Old Testament is filled with prayers used by the community. The Psalms were written for use in worship. In the Gospels we find Jesus participating in the worship life of the community (Luke 4:16). He probably recited the *Shema* (Deuteronomy 6:4) twice a day, as did other pious Jews, and prayed the other prayers that were in common use. In the Epistles we find examples of prayers used by the early church (2 Corinthians 13:14, Philippians 2:5-11, 1 Timothy 1:17, Jude 24-25).

Finally, written prayers give us a structure upon which to hang our private prayers. We begin with the words of others, and before we know it we are praying our own words. As C. S. Lewis commented about the choice between "ready-made prayers and one's own words. . . . It does not matter very much who first put them together. If they are our own words they will soon, by unavoidable repetition, harden into a formula. If they are someone else's, we shall continually pour into them our own meaning."[2]

65

DISCUSSION   **5 MINUTES**

4. What has your experience been when it comes to using
written prayers?

PRAYER EXERCISE: PREPARATION   **10-15 MINUTES**

Today's exercise has two parts to it. First you will write a prayer
of your own around a particular theme. Then you will use that
prayer as part of a service of prayer, based on the themes of the
Lord's Prayer. The prayers you will use are drawn from the rich
legacy of prayer left to us by men and women through the ages.

The most common written prayer is probably the Lord's
Prayer (also known as the "Our Father" or *Paternoster*). The
disciples asked Jesus, "Teach us to pray." In response, Jesus
gave them a model prayer in which he addressed the major
themes of prayer (Matthew 6:9-13). Here is the version in the
Episcopal *Book of Common Prayer*:

> *Our Father, who art in heaven,*
> *hallowed be thy Name,*
> *thy kingdom come,*
> *thy will be done, on earth as it is in heaven.*
> *Give us this day our daily bread.*
> *And forgive us our trespasses,*
> *as we forgive those who trespass against us.*
> *And lead us not into temptation,*
> *but deliver us from evil.*
> *For thine is the kingdom,*
> *and the power, and the glory,*
> *for ever and ever. Amen.*[3]

There are many ways to analyze this simple but profound
prayer. One is by noting the three major movements in the
prayer.

❖ Dependence, blessing, and thanksgiving (the first four lines)
❖ Petition: give/forgive/deliver (the next five lines)
❖ Adoration and contemplation (final three lines)

The Lord's Prayer will be the basis for your prayer time together. Read over "A Service of Prayer" on the next page. Look carefully at each type of prayer, and choose one type that you will write. (If you are working on your own, you can write all three types.)

On your own in silence, write a short prayer on one of these themes that you can offer to God during the prayer service. The prayer types from which to choose are:

❖ prayer of dependence
❖ prayer of blessing or thanksgiving
❖ petition for the meeting of needs
❖ petition for forgiveness (confession of sins)
❖ petition for deliverance
❖ prayer of adoration and contemplation

A SERVICE OF PRAYER   20-35 MINUTES

Begin by praying the Lord's Prayer (see page 66). If you are
with a group, pray in unison.

Confess your *dependence* on God, who is, indeed, "Our Father,"
using this ancient prayer of Thomas à Kempis (1380-1471).

> *Grant me, O most sweet and loving Jesus, to rest in Thee
> above every creature, above all health and beauty, above all
> glory and honor, above all power and dignity, above all
> knowledge and subtlety, above all riches and arts, above all
> joy and exultation, above all fame and praise, above all sweet-
> ness and consolation, above all hope and promise, above all
> desert and desire, above all gifts and presents which Thou art
> able to bestow or infuse, above all joy and gladness which the
> mind is capable of receiving and feeling; finally, above Angels
> and Archangels, and above all the hosts of Heaven, above all
> things visible and invisible, and above all that falls short of
> Thyself, O Thou, my God.[4]*

If you have written a prayer of dependence, pray it aloud now.
(In a group, all those who have written prayers of dependence
will pray them now.)

Offer blessing and thanksgiving to God by saying Psalm 100
below (in unison, if in a group).

> *Shout for joy to the LORD, all the earth.*
> > *Worship the LORD with gladness;*
> > *come before him with joyful songs.*
> *Know that the LORD is God.*
> > *It is he who made us, and we are his;*
> > *we are his people, the sheep of his pasture.*
> *Enter his gates with thanksgiving*
> > *and his courts with praise;*
> > *give thanks to him and praise his name.*
> *For the LORD is good and his love endures forever;*
> > *his faithfulness continues through all generations.*

If you have written a prayer of blessing or thanksgiving, pray it aloud now.

Now move to the prayers of petition, beginning with a prayer in which you ask God to "give us our daily bread. . . ."

> *Lord God, we thank you for all the good things of your provid-*
> *ing, and we pray for the time when people everywhere shall*
> *have the abundant life of your will, revealed to us in Jesus*
> *Christ, your Son, our Lord.*
> —George Appleton (editor, *Oxford Book of Prayer*)

Pray aloud in your own words, briefly, asking God to meet your needs. Use a prayer you have written, or express your needs spontaneously.

Move to the second petition, in which you ask God to "forgive us . . ." using the General Confession from the Episcopal *Book of Common Prayer*:

> *Most merciful God,*
> *we confess that we have sinned against you*
> *in thought, word, and deed,*
> *by what we have done,*
> *and by what we have left undone.*
> *We have not loved you with our whole heart;*
> *we have not loved our neighbors as ourselves.*
> *We are truly sorry and we humbly repent.*
> *For the sake of your Son Jesus Christ,*
> *have mercy on us and forgive us;*
> *that we may delight in your will,*
> *and walk in your ways,*
> *to the glory of your Name. Amen.*[5]

Offer your prayer of repentance if you have written one. Then silently confess your sin, asking God for forgiveness.

Conclude this section of prayer with the final petition in which you ask God to "deliver us . . ." using St. Augustine's prayer.

*Blessed are all thy Saints, O God and King, who have traveled
over the tempestuous sea of this mortal life, and have made the
harbor of peace and felicity. Watch over us who are still in our
dangerous voyage; and remember such as lie exposed to the
rough storms of trouble and temptations. Frail is our vessel,
and the ocean is wide; but as in thy mercy thou has set our
course, so steer the vessel of our life toward the everlasting
shore of peace, and bring us at length to the quiet haven of our
heart's desire, where thou, O our God, are blessed, and livest
and reignest for ever and ever.*

—Augustine (354-430)

Offer your petition for deliverance if you have written one.

Offer your prayer of adoration if you have written one.

Conclude with this prayer of adoration:

Gracious God,
We love you because you first loved us.
We wandered far from you,
yet you pursued us.
We turned aside from your ways,
yet you forgave us.
We forgot who you were,
yet you whispered your name to us.
May we be given grace to love you
with even a fraction of the love you give us. Amen.

If you are meeting with a group, your leader will conclude your
prayer time by offering the benediction of Jude 24-25:

*To him who is able to keep you from falling and to present you
before his glorious presence without fault and with great joy—
to the only God our Savior be glory, majesty, power and
authority, through Jesus Christ our Lord, before all ages, now
and forevermore! Amen.*

Discuss the experience with your group or in your journal.[6]

REFLECTION

God Gives Us Our Prayers

I used to think prayer was mostly up to me. I would come before God praising and thanking him for who he is and for all he had done for me. I would offer confession. Then I would get into the long list of requests I had for God. This was the real heart of my prayer: the tasks upon which I hoped God would focus his power.

There is nothing wrong with such prayer. Any prayer is better than no prayer (which is our usual state). But in recent years I find that my prayer is richest when I begin by listening, not speaking. "Lord, what would you have me pray?" Thoughts come to me; people present themselves; a passage of Scripture comes to mind; an idea occurs to me. When I use these promptings I find that I pray with focus and confidence. Sometimes I write out these prayers. Mostly I just offer them back to God.

So what is prayer in the end? Is it some sort of urgent pleading with God to deal with an issue? Or is it an offering back to God of what he desires? I suspect prayer is both but mainly the latter.

Does God need our prayers? Yes and no. God is God and can run the universe quite well without us. But God has chosen to involve us (for reasons we cannot fathom) in the running of the universe. Or at least God wants us to participate in some way (beyond our understanding) in the affairs located in our small corner of the planet.

For a period of time in my twenties I found it hard to pray because it seemed that if God were sovereign (which I believed) and if God were omniscient (which I also believed), whether I prayed or not did not matter. What happened would happen. Nothing could frustrate the will of God. And besides, God already knew what would happen. Why bother to pray? My mind prevented my prayer. But eventually I came to see that God urges us to pray. Scripture insists upon it. Somehow it matters that we pray—even if we don't understand why. C. S. Lewis was a great help to me as I wrestled with the logic of intercessory prayer (see his *Letters to Malcolm: Chiefly on Prayer*).

But now I see that God gives us prayers he wants us to pray. Psalm 37:4 says, "Delight yourself in the LORD and he will give you the desires of your heart." I think this verse is true in two senses. The very desires we have, when we delight in the Lord, come *from* God (are these the prayers God gives us?); and these desires are granted us by the Lord because they are God's desires (is this why prayer is answered?).

But to pray the prayers God wants us to pray, we need to be in a place where we touch him. In that place, we can hear most clearly the voice of God, as distinct from the voice of our needs and wishes or the voice of our culture. This brings us back to the fundamental reality of prayer: it is not so much what we do as where we are. In the end, to pray is simply to be at that still point where God is.

At the center of our being we are in contact with God. The Holy Spirit is alive within us, uttering prayers and groanings too deep to be captured by mere words. But our heart—which is the ancient word for the center of our being—is hidden from us. It is covered with layer upon layer of debris. The aim of all our prayer techniques is to penetrate through this encrustation to the hidden center and so be in touch with the ceaseless prayer that flows from this core.

When we open ourselves to God who is in us, prayer is easy. Prayer becomes life itself. At this center point there is peace and harmony—with God, with ourselves, with others. But it is a long and hard way back to this center point. We need each other in this process. We need all the help we can get: written prayers by those who have walked this journey before us; ways of meditation; the focus that the Psalms bring to our prayer; the guidance of all the prayer methods developed through the centuries. It is a long road but, in the end, it is the road that brings the kind of spiritual wholeness we crave.

WEEKLY EXERCISES

Each day: If you can, begin to explore what is available in books of prayers. Your church may have its own prayer book, and that would be a good place to start. I also recommend *A Diary of Private Prayer* by John Baillie, who was a professor of

Divinity at the University of Edinburgh. This book contains prayers for each morning and evening during a month. The prayers are interspersed between blank pages where you can record your own prayers and prayer requests. I have used this small prayer book off and on for over thirty-five years, and it remains fresh and vital for me. The depth of Baillie's wisdom and piety shine through in these prayers, which have the uncanny knack of capturing just the issues we are facing.

Then there is *The Oxford Book of Prayer*, which is a collection of prayers from around the world, organized into categories that allow the reader to find the right prayer for the right occasion. I have used this resource for years and am constantly finding new prayers that speak to my condition and stimulate my meditation. You will be amazed at the range and power of prayers composed by learned theologians, obscure monks, and small children.

You will find these books helpful to you in composing the suggested prayers for this week's exercise. Your task is to write prayers that might be used on family occasions. Robert Webber's *The Book of Family Prayer* (Nelson, 1986) also may help you in this process.

Day one: Grace. Write a prayer that can be used at mealtime to thank God for his provision.

Day two: Bed time. Write a prayer that can be used with children as they are put to bed.

Day three: Morning. Write a prayer with which you can begin a new day.

Day four: Christmas. Write a prayer for use at the family meal on Christmas Day. Or write four prayers that can be used during the four weeks of Advent (the weeks before Christmas).

Day five: Easter. Write a prayer for use at the family meal on Easter. Or write prayers that can be used during Lent (the six weeks that lead up to Easter).

Notes

1. *The Oxford Book of Prayer*, edited by George Appleton (London: Oxford University Press, 1985), p. 225. St. John Chrysostom lived in the fourth century, and this liturgy is used by the Eastern Orthodox Church.
2. C. S. Lewis, *Letters to Malcolm: Chiefly on Prayer* (New York: Harcourt Brace & World, 1963), p. 11.
3. *The Book of Common Prayer*, p. 364.
4. This prayer and the others that follow can be found in *The Oxford Book of Prayer*: Thomas à Kempis, #141, p. 54; George Appleton, # 339, p. 105; Augustine, #413, p. 123.
5. *The Book of Common Prayer*, p. 352.
6. Please notice that given the nature of the small group exercise there is no "Closing Prayer".

SESSION SEVEN

Prayer of Distress

PSALMS 42 AND 43

Group Note:
Leader's Notes for this session can be found on page 110.

Overview

How do we pray when we are down? So far it may seem as if prayer is only for upbeat, motivated, and joy-filled people. But life is not always easy. Can we pray when we are unhappy, discouraged, fragmented, and sad?

The Psalms show us that prayer is possible in all circumstances. In fact, the Psalms reflect the whole range of human emotion: sadness, joy, fear, hope, despair, love, hatred, anger, and awe. In this session we will examine two psalms that express the experience of distress. The psalmist is discouraged and sad. He longs for God; he feels rejected by God; he is overwhelmed by his enemies. Yet his strong trust in God shines through his pain. We, too, need to learn how to pray in the midst of our distress.

Pray the following prayer taken from Psalms 42 and 43. Then ask God to give you insight in this session into how to pray when life gets tough.

As the deer pants for streams of water,
        so my soul pants for you, O God.
My soul thirsts for God, for the living God. . . .
By day the LORD directs his love,
        at night his song is with me—
        a prayer to the God of my life. . . .
Send forth your light and your truth,
        let them guide me;
let them bring me to your holy mountain,
        to the place where you dwell.
Then will I go to the altar of God,
        to God, my joy and my delight.
I will praise you with the harp,
        O God, my God.
Why are you downcast, O my soul?
        Why so disturbed within me?
Put your hope in God,
        for I will yet praise him,
        my Savior and my God.

OPEN   20-30 MINUTES

Getting in Trouble

We all do it: we get in trouble. Kids in particular seem to be trouble-prone. What kind of kid were you when you were growing up?

1. What is one of the mischievous things you did as a child? What happened as a result?

2. Were you the kind of kid who got into mischief, avoided mischief, or just never got caught?

TEXT   5 MINUTES

Most scholars believe that Psalms 42 and 43 are, in fact, a single psalm. They share a common refrain (see Psalms 42:5,11; 43:5) and the issues raised in Psalm 42 are resolved in Psalm 43.

This double psalm is a lament. To lament is to grieve deeply; it is to mourn. Because we all experience trials and suffering, it is a great comfort to know that we can bring our laments to God and that God will respond. In our trials we come to realize our ultimate helplessness and deep need of God. In fact, it is in our distress that we often find God. The first prayer some people utter is, "O God, help me." As we encounter our own insufficiency, we discover the sufficiency of God.

These psalms are divided into three parts, each concluded by the common refrain. Part 1 (Psalm 42:1-4) is a lament that might be called, "The Drought." Part 2 (Psalm 42:6-10) is also a lament and might be called, "The Depths." Part 3 (Psalm 43:1-4) is a prayer that might be entitled, "The Release."[1] The movement through these three parts goes from deep despair to confident hope.

[1]As the deer pants for streams of water,
    so my soul pants for you, O God.
[2]My soul thirsts for God, for the living God.
    When can I go and meet with God?
[3]My tears have been my
    food day and night,
while men say to me all day long,
    "Where is your God?"
[4]These things I remember
    as I pour out my soul:
how I used to go with the multitude,
    leading the procession to the house of God,
with shouts of joy and thanksgiving
    among the festive throng.

[5]Why are you downcast, O my soul?
    Why so disturbed within me?
Put your hope in God,
    for I will yet praise him,
    my Savior and [6]my God.

My soul is downcast within me;
    therefore I will remember you

from the land of the Jordan,
     the heights of Hermon—from Mount Mizar.
⁷Deep calls to deep
     in the roar of your waterfalls;
all your waves and breakers
     have swept over me.

⁸By day the LORD directs his love,
     at night his song is with me—
     a prayer to the God of my life.

⁹I say to God my Rock,
     "Why have you forgotten me?
Why must I go about mourning,
     oppressed by the enemy?"
¹⁰My bones suffer mortal agony
     as my foes taunt me,
saying to me all day long,
     "Where is your God?"

¹¹Why are you downcast, O my soul?
     Why so disturbed within me?
Put your hope in God,
     for I will yet praise him,
     my Savior and my God. (Psalm 42)

¹Vindicate me, O God,
     and plead my cause against an ungodly nation;
     rescue me from deceitful and wicked men.
²You are God my stronghold.
     Why have you rejected me?
Why must I go about mourning,
     oppressed by the enemy?
³Send forth your light and your truth,
     let them guide me;
let them bring me to your holy mountain,
     to the place where you dwell.
⁴Then will I go to the altar of God,
     to God, my joy and my delight.

I will praise you with the harp,
O God, my God.

⁵Why are you downcast, O my soul?
Why so disturbed within me?
Put your hope in God,
for I will yet praise him,
my Savior and my God. (Psalm 43)

ANALYSIS   **10-15 MINUTES**
3. Examine the first lament (Psalm 42:1-4).

a. What images does the psalmist use to describe his longing?
b. What is the nature of his plight as expressed here?
c. What does he remember, and how does this memory
serve him?

4. Examine the second lament (Psalm 42:6-10).

a. What are the psalmist's good memories, and how do they
serve him?
b. What are his difficult experiences? How do they add to
your understanding of his plight?

5. Examine his prayer (Psalm 43:1-4).

a. In what ways is the tone of this section different from the
previous two?
b. What does the psalmist ask of God? How does this asking affect his state of being?

6. Examine the refrain (Psalm 42:5,11; 43:5).

a. What is his plight?
b. What is his confidence?

APPLICATION   **15-30 MINUTES**

7. What aspects of life make people downcast and disturbed ("down in the dumps and crying the blues"[2])? Think about not only your own experience but that of the world in general.

8. Where is God when we are in trouble? Think about your own experiences of hard times.

9. Based on this study, what kind of prayer can we pray when we find ourselves in the midst of pain and difficulty?

The following prayer by Thomas Fuller (1608-1661) addresses the question of suffering, not from within the experience of suffering (as in a psalm of lament) but in anticipation that it will come.

> Lord, teach me the art of patience whilst I am well, and give me the use of it when I am sick. In that day either lighten my burden or strengthen my back. Make me, who so often in my health have discovered my weakness presuming on my own strength, to be strong in my sickness when I solely rely on thy assistance.[3]

Now write your own prayer of lament on the top of the next page. Use the form found in Psalms 42 and 43: begin by pouring out in graphic terms that which saddens you (your own plight or the plight of the world); then express your confidence in God amidst the problem; and end with a prayer asking for God's provision in the midst of your lament.

Use this space to write your prayer.

CLOSING PRAYER   10 MINUTES

If you are meeting with a group, conclude this session by dis-
cussing together the why and how of the prayer you wrote.
Then pray these prayers with one another, using Thomas
Fuller's prayer as part of this experience.

WEEKLY EXERCISES

Each day: This week, pray for the needs of the world. Do this by taking a different theme each day, reflecting on that issue as you understand and experience it. Then write a prayer that offers the issue to God using the prayer of lament format: vivid description of the problem; expression of confidence in God's provision; general petition to God.

Day one: Illness. Pray for those who are sick, as well as for those who seek to alleviate illness and/or care for the sick.

Day two: Famine. Pray for those who don't get enough to eat, as well as for those who seek to alleviate famine and provide the kind of aid that results in better crops.

Day three: Disaster. Pray for those who are suffering in the aftermath of natural disaster, such as flood, storm, or fire, and for those who respond to disasters, providing aid and comfort.

Day four: Psychological pain. Pray for those who are suffering from depression, loneliness, mental disorder, and addiction, as well as for those who offer relief, understanding, and guidance.

Day five: Spiritual distress. Pray for those who feel lost in the universe, cut off from God and from meaning, and for those who minister to them with words of life.

BACKGROUND NOTES

It is important to understand the character of lamentation in order to interpret properly the psalms of lament. First, the psalmist details his or the nation's distress, often dramatically. "My wounds fester and are loathsome. . . . My back is filled with searing pain; there is no health in my body. I am feeble and utterly crushed. I groan in anguish of heart" (Psalm 38:5-8). We are almost embarrassed by what seems excessive self-pity. But the strong language contrasts with the psalmist's utter confidence in God. "You are a shield around me, O LORD, my Glorious One, who lifts up my head. . . . I will not fear the tens of thousands drawn up against me on every side" (Psalm 3:3,6).

Both the lament and the confidence are expressed extrava-
gantly. This technique encourages us to express freely and fully
the depth of our trial and also to depend utterly upon a God
who hears our cries.

The final element in the psalms of lament is petition: those
requests we make of God based on our problem and God's
character. In most of these psalms the requests are general.
They don't tell God what to do specifically; rather they trust
that God will do right. Magic tells God what to do; prayer lets
God deal with things in his own way.

Many of the laments are corporate, not individual. The cry
and the faith are on behalf of the community or nation. So, too,
as we use the psalms of lament as our prayers, we can pray
them on behalf of the suffering world.

Psalm 42:1-4: The Psalm opens with a vivid image: a deeply
thirsty deer who can find no water in that desert land. The
psalmist uses this as an image for his own deep thirst for God.
He then remembers times of joyous worship when he went up
to the temple with all the other pilgrims. God was present in
those festivals and he longs for this to be true once again. But,
alas, his soul remains downcast. His thirst has not yet been sat-
isfied.

The tone of this first lament is deep discouragement. As we
pray it is important to name fully and clearly what we face. We
do not have to draw back from our pain. We need to present it
to God in all its intensity.

Psalm 42:5: This refrain is used three times. Each time it brings
to an end a section of the psalm. It is the core of psalm: the
recognition of one's pain and a statement of hope in God
because of who he is. The refrain defines for us the structure of
our own prayers of distress. We begin by stating vividly and in
detail the exact nature of our problem. We don't need to leave
anything out; God wants to hear it all. Then we move to the
core confidence in our lives and define the nature of our trust
in a completely dependable God. We end with petition, which
is not so much a detailed list of requests as it is a request for
help to make it through the trial.

Psalm 42:6-10: In this second lament the psalmist determines to "remember" God. God is absent to him at that moment so he will cast back his memory to those moments in the past when God was alive, vivid, and active (as symbolized by places where he had met God). But memory fails him and what he does recall is chaos as symbolized in waterfalls and waves that sweep over him. He then catches a glimpse of God and the love that surrounds him. But that memory is swept away and the reality of his plight comes back. He does know though that even in the midst of such battering, God is like a rock: solid and able to withstand even the power of wave. Still, the most vivid aware-ness is of his plight: his grief, his oppression by others, his physical pain, the taunts which mock his trust in God. It feels like God has forgotten him. Twice he has remembered God in the past and yet he remains downcast.

In times of silence it is our memory of what we have expe-rienced of God that will enable us to declare our confidence in God. But we are not always successful in remembering those moments when God was present. We may be reminded, instead, of the waves of pain and despair that seem to engulf us. God may once have been present but now it feels as though like he has forgotten us. God can accept such swings of feeling on our part. He does not ask us to pretend. Sometimes we sim-ply have to go through the pain before we can find the hope.

Psalm 43:1-4: Now the psalmist's internal dialogue with himself is transformed into external dialogue with God. Lament has turned into prayer. There is no help from memory. Help must come from God. He begins by asking God to take up his case and be a defense counsel for him as he faces his enemies. He then asks for guidance as well as defense. It will be God's light and truth that mark the way out of his darkness. It will show the path back to God (to the place where God dwells and to the altar where he is worshipped).

Notes

1. These three titles are taken from *Psalms 1-72* by Derek Kidner (Downers Grove, Ill.: InterVarsity, 1973), pp. 165-167.
2. Eugene Peterson, *The Message: Psalms*, Psalm 42:11.
3. *The Oxford Book of Prayer*, p. 130.

Prayer Styles and Personality

PRAYING FROM WHO YOU ARE

Group Note:
Leader's Notes for this session can be found on page 110.

Overview

There is no one way to pray. This is fortunate because personalities differ so much. Different prayer styles fit different personalities. Unfortunately, individual churches or denominations tend to focus on a single style of prayer. If such an approach to prayer fits you, that's great; if not, prayer can become difficult, boring, or remote. In this session we will explore four different prayer styles that fit the four basic human temperaments plus a fifth style that fits almost everyone.[1] The hope is that you will discover the style of prayer that resonates most deeply with who you are. Pray this prayer aloud:

Lord God, ruler of the universe, thank you that you have made each of us in a unique way. We bless you for the awesome diversity of your creative power. Help us in this session to discern style of prayer that best fits who you have made each of us to be. Give us new ways to know you, to respond to you, to hear you, and to love you. We pray in Jesus' name. Amen.

OPEN   **20-30 MINUTES**
Preferences
We all have them. In one sense, the sum of our preferences
makes us who we are. What do you prefer?

1. After a long day of work, how would you prefer to spend
   the evening? (Check only one.)

   ❏ throw a party for 50 people
   ❏ sit on the deck and watch the stars
   ❏ read in front of a comfortable fire
   ❏ go to a concert
   ❏ watch two videos
   ❏ attend a small group session
   ❏ have dinner with a few close friends
   ❏ other:

2. How would you plan that evening? (Check all that apply.)

   ❏ just let it happen
   ❏ let someone else plan it
   ❏ make a list of what I need
   ❏ read a book about how to do it
   ❏ I'd be open to something else happening
   ❏ other:

3. What do you think about the whole idea of personality
   types?

DEFINING YOUR TEMPERAMENT   15 MINUTES

People have different personality types and each personality type has a preferred way of praying. Knowing your preferred prayer style will help you organize your ongoing prayer activities. Of course, everyone should take advantage of all the different ways of praying because each opens up new insights and new ways to approach God. But if there is one style that resonates most deeply with you, you will want to use it regularly.

You will sample four prayer styles in this session. In order to discern which style is most likely to suit you, you need to know your Myers-Briggs personality type. The Myers-Briggs Type Indicator is a popular test instrument, so you may already know which four-letter combination defines your personality type. If so, you can help others in your group (if you are meeting with a group) as they reflect on where they fit into this typology.

Because many people don't know their types, begin by doing an unscientific "test" that will point you in the right direction. Take a moment and answer the following three questions. They should define your temperament.

A Test for Temperament
  4. With which one of these four New Testament characters do you most closely identify? (That is, which person are you most like?) Take into account the short description of each person.

  A. *James*, who understood that duty flows from faith

  B. *Paul*, who kept envisioning new possibilities for the emerging church

  C. *Peter*, who as a man of action used his trouble-shooting abilities to reconcile various elements in the church

  D. *John*, who as a contemplative helped us understand what it meant that the Word had become flesh[2]

5. Which type of prayer do you most enjoy? (Choose one only.)

   A. Imagining myself to be a participant in one of the Gospel stories, hearing Jesus' words addressed to me, and responding to what he says

   B. Reading a psalm, listening to what each phrase says about my life, and offering my reflections to God

   C. Walking in a beautiful forest, thanking God for what I see and experience, and talking with him about whatever occurs to me

   D. Thinking about my friends and family, writing out their needs, and then praying to God about each need, one by one

6. Which one of these four descriptions most accurately describes you?

   A. Those who have this temperament are dutiful people, with a deep sense of obligation and a desire to be useful. They prefer giving rather than receiving, are practical, have a strong work ethic, are committed to order and structure, and have a strong sense of tradition. They are caretakers who often are overworked.

   B. "[Those who have this temperament] . . . are usually creative, optimistic, verbal, persuasive, outspoken, good at both writing and speaking. They have a great need for self-expression and communicate with others easily. . . . They find it difficult to handle negative criticism and . . . blossom under affirmation."[3] They are natural pilgrims who want to become all that God has for them.

   C. Those who have this temperament are action-oriented. They are impulsive and free spirited; they chafe at rules. "They are flexible, easy to get along with, open-minded, adaptable, willing to change their position. . . . They live very much in the present without concern either for the past or future. . . . They are always looking for something new, new places to go, new things to do."[4] They thrive on excitement and activity, and are great in dealing with crises.

D. Those who have this temperament are known for their logical minds that approach problems in a systematic fashion. They like complexity and the challenge it brings. They have a thirst for truth and a desire for control. They hunger for knowledge and perfection; they want to know the truth and to do it perfectly. They tend to be serious in their pursuit of competency.

Which temperament are you? If this "test" works out the way it is supposed to, you will have circled the same letter in each of the three questions. (If you did not, go with the results of the third question, which contains the most information.) The "answers" to the test, along with the preferred prayer style, are as follows:

A = SJ—Ignatian prayer
B = NF—Augustinian prayer
C = SP—Franciscan prayer
D = NT—Thomistic prayer

PRAYER EXERCISE   15 MINUTES

You will do the following exercise on your own. If you are
meeting with a group, you may want to scatter throughout the
meeting place, or you could just sit together in silence. Find
the type of prayer that matches your temperament and do the
exercise. You will have fifteen minutes. (If you are with a
group, your leader will call you back together when the time
is up.)

Ignatian Prayer (SJ)

Ignatian prayer fits the SJ temperament. It was developed in the
sixteenth century, but in fact, its roots are much older than
that. It can be traced back to Old Testament styles of prayer in
which the focus is on remembering (remembering the great
events done by God on behalf of Israel). St. Ignatius of Loyola
(the founder of the Jesuits) taught his followers to project
themselves back into past events, to relive these biblical events
in all their detail, and to participate in the events themselves. In
this way a person brings the presence of Jesus into the here and
now. Ignatius urged people to use all five senses during their
imaginative journeys back to seminal biblical events. The key
process in this form of prayer is *projection* back into the original scene by means of *sense-based imagination*. This is the
method of prayer you used in session four.

Do the following Ignatian prayer exercise.

❖ Read aloud softly to yourself Luke 10:30-35, the story of
the good Samaritan.

> *Jesus said: "A man was going down from Jerusalem to
> Jericho, when he fell into the hands of robbers. They
> stripped him of his clothes, beat him and went away,
> leaving him half dead. A priest happened to be going
> down the same road, and when he saw the man, he
> passed by on the other side. So too, a Levite, when he
> came to the place and saw him, passed by on the other
> side. But a Samaritan, as he traveled, came where the
> man was; and when he saw him, he took pity on him. He
> went to him and bandaged his wounds, pouring on oil*

and wine. Then he put the man on his own donkey, took him to an inn and took care of him. The next day he took out two silver coins and gave them to the innkeeper. 'Look after him,' he said, 'and when I return, I will reimburse you for any extra expense you may have.'"

❖ Project yourself back into the story in your imagination using the following prayer guide. Be alert to what you see, hear, touch, smell, or even taste. You may wish to make notes as you pray, or you might prefer simply to remain in the atmosphere of prayer.

Read over again, slowly, the story of the good Samaritan. First, imagine yourself as the priest who passes by on the other side of the road. What reasons could you give for refusing to get involved? Second, imagine yourself as that person who fell among the robbers and was left half dead by the side of the road. What did you think and feel as people passed you by and refused your cries for help? What did you experience when the Samaritan came to your aid? Third, imagine yourself as the good Samaritan. What did you think and feel and experience as you saw the injured person and went to his rescue? Finally, envision situations today in which you could be called upon to act like the good Samaritan.[5]

Augustinian Prayer (NF)
Augustinian prayer fits the NF temperament. It was developed for the convents and monasteries in North Africa served by St. Augustine. It calls upon people to use creative imagination to transpose the words of Scripture to their own situations. Try to imagine that God is speaking these words to you at this moment in time. Seek to discern their meaning for your life. Augustinians practice the prayer of transposition: "Lord, what do these words mean to me in my present situation?"

Extroverted NFs use these insights as the basis for conversation with others. Introverted NFs record their discoveries in their journals. The key process in this form of prayer is

transposition whereby through *creative imagination* the words of Scripture are applied to contemporary situations.
Do the following Augustinian prayer exercise.

❖ Get out a sheet of paper on which you can write (which you can later put in your journal).

❖ Read the following passage from John 15:9-17. As you do so, imagine Jesus speaking these words directly to you. What do they mean to you? Repeat to yourself those words and phrases of Jesus that have special value to you; savor them lovingly, joyfully. Write them down. Memorize them. Write your reflections on this experience.

> *"As the Father has loved me, so have I loved you. Now remain in my love. If you obey my commands, you will remain in my love, just as I have obeyed my Father's commands and remain in his love. I have told you this so that my joy may be in you and that your joy may be complete. My command is this: Love each other as I have loved you. Greater love has no one than this, that he lay down his life for his friends. You are my friends if you do what I command. I no longer call you servants, because a servant does not know his master's business. Instead, I have called you friends, for everything that I learned from my Father I have made known to you. You did not choose me, but I chose you and appointed you to go and bear fruit —fruit that will last. Then the Father will give you whatever you ask in my name. This is my command: Love each other."*

Franciscan Prayer (SP)

Franciscan prayer fits the SP temperament. St. Francis of Assisi was a spontaneous, nature-loving man who found God in the freedom of poverty and movement. Franciscan prayer is free-flowing and spontaneous, filled with praise and conversation with God. Such prayer extends over into action. It may take place out-of-doors as the person meditates on God's creation, finding God's presence in nature. It is expressed not just in words but in song, movement, and art. Franciscan prayer is celebratory, filled with love, expressed in informal words. The world is the SP Bible. However, SPs do love the Gospels with their accounts of the life of Jesus. The key process in this form of prayer is *spontaneity* that is alert to the movement of the Spirit.

Do the following Franciscan prayer exercise.

❖ Get out a sheet of paper on which you can write if you want.

❖ Think of the person you most love in this world. Ask yourself: How can I see the presence of God in that person? "Spend some time praising and thanking God for giving so much goodness, beauty, grace, and so on to that person. Spend some time thanking God for the gift of love whereby you are able to love that person and that person is able to love you."[6]

❖ Sketch an image, draw a doodle, or make a symbol that captures what you see of God in that person. Or write a song or poem that does the same thing.

Thomistic Prayer (NT)

Thomistic prayer fits the NT temperament. It reflects the spiritual perspective of St. Thomas Aquinas, the great medieval scholar and theologian. This prayer moves in an orderly manner from cause to effect. It is based on rational thought that seeks to know the truth about the subject being considered. "This type of prayer . . . is logical, rational, discursive meditation whereby the intellect leads from one proposition to another until a logical conclusion is drawn in the form of some resolution or ethical demand."[7] "One looks for new insights from God concerning the virtue to be practiced, the fault to be overcome, the religious practice to be perfected."[8] In this form of prayer, a person picks an issue and examines it extensively, ending with new resolution. By means of active imagination, those truths derived from the analysis of Scripture are integrated into a life of holiness. The key process in this form of prayer is *thoughtful reflection* that seeks to understand the ways of God.

Do the following Thomistic prayer exercise.

❖ Get out a sheet of paper on which to make notes.

❖ Consider Matthew 5:23-24:

> *"If you are offering your gift at the altar and there remember that your brother has something against you, leave your gift there in front of the altar. First go and be reconciled to your brother; then come and offer your gift."*

"Are you willing to take this command of Jesus literally? Do you believe that it is more important to be reconciled with your brothers and sisters than it is to [take communion] on Sunday? At present is there anyone in your life not reconciled with you? Have you tried to become reconciled with him/her? Have you tried as much as you should? As much as God would want you to do? Do you really love that person who is not reconciled to you? What more can you do to become reconciled with those who have something against you? Even if the 'thing against you' is not real (for example, imaginary) is there anything you should do to bring about an understanding between the two of you?"[9]

❖ As you think through all of this, do so in the presence of God, offering your meditation to God and resolving to hear what God has to say to you in this matter.

Benedictine Prayer (All temperaments)

Benedictine prayer is useful for all temperaments. Introduced in the fourth century by John Cassian and later described by St. Benedict in his monastic *Rule*, this form of prayer is called *lectio divina* or sacred reading.[10] It is a four part process:

❖ reading/listening (*lectio*), in which you read a passage of

Scripture aloud slowly, noticing the word or phrase that especially strikes you as having meaning for you

❖ meditating (*meditatio*), in which you repeat the word or phrase aloud and make connections to your life

❖ praying (*oratio*), in which you offer these meditations back to God as prayer, asking for his guidance

❖ contemplating (*contemplatio*), in which you simply rest in God's presence

DISCUSSION   **15-25 MINUTES**

Use these questions to spark a discussion (if you are meeting with a group) or for reflection in your journal (if you are working alone).

7. What good things came out of the prayer exercise for you? What new things did you learn about prayer?

8. Was this prayer style a match for your own tendencies?

9. What aspects of the prayer styles you didn't select seemed appealing or helpful to you?

10. a. Thinking back over the weeks you've spent in this study guide, what experience of prayer stands out as the most memorable?

    b. What new insights have you learned about prayer?

11. If you have been meeting with a group, what have you appreciated most about the other members of your group?

12. If you are meeting with a group, talk about where you might go from here.

    ❑ Study together another book in the Spiritual Formation series.
    ❑ Continue to meet to pray together.
    ❑ Start new small groups in which to teach others the art of prayer.
    ❑ Disband as a group but have a reunion meal in a month.
    ❑ Say good-bye and join a new group.

CLOSING PRAYER   5 MINUTES

End by praying the well-known prayer of St. Francis of Assisi
(1181-1226).

> *Lord, make me a instrument of your peace.*
> *Where there is hatred, let me sow love,*
> *Where there is injury, pardon;*
> *Where there is doubt, faith;*
> *Where there is despair, hope;*
> *Where there is darkness, light;*
> *Where there is sadness, joy.*
> *O divine Master, Grant that I may not so much seek*
> *To be consoled, as to console,*
> *To be understood, as to understand,*
> *To be loved, as to love,*
> *For it is in giving that we receive;*
> *It is in pardoning that we are pardoned;*
> *It is in dying that we are born to eternal life.*[11]

REFLECTION

Finding Space for Prayer in the Gaps of Life

We are all too busy. This seems to be a fact of modern life. It is
no good decrying the fact that we do not have enough time. It
is hard to do much about this reality unless we opt out of life
as we know it.

There are some options for finding more time: we could
watch less television (the average American watches over
twenty hours each week); we could hire others to do the time-
consuming tasks of maintaining our increasingly complex
homes (but this costs money that many of us do not have); we
could wake up earlier in the morning (but recent studies indicate that a majority of Americans are sleep deprived); we could
cut down on leisure activities (but lack of rest contributes to
the high level of stress in our society); we could restrict family
and social time (but isn't life meant to be all about relationships, especially with family?). The fact is that finding more
time is beyond most of us.

So how do we cultivate a spiritual life on top of all this?
How do we pray regularly?

I think we must notice the gaps that exist in the daily routine of life and use these for prayer. I have in mind:

* the commute to work
* the times we are on hold while our computer boots up or someone takes our call
* lunch hour
* the time between climbing in bed and falling asleep
* canceled appointments
* showering and getting dressed

There are many gaps in our schedules. Most are small; a few are big; occasionally we have unexpected time. If we can learn to recognize these as moments for prayer, we just might beat the time crunch that threatens the vitality of our spiritual sides.

I tried an experiment last year. For the first time in many years I had to commute to work. The challenge was how to pay attention to my driving on a crowded Los Angeles freeway and use the time to pray. This is some of what I found.

* Driving is the first priority, especially when the freeway is crowded (which is most days in L.A.). Whatever I did required that I keep my eyes on the road (no bowed head here!), my hands on the steering wheel (no raised hands either), and sufficient focus so that I could respond to the ever-changing freeway conditions. This meant that I had to choose my prayer exercises carefully.

* I always began by praying, "Lord, guide my driving and protect me and others on this busy freeway."

* Praying aloud helped a lot. It kept me focused. It also helped keep my mind from wandering. And it felt more like a conversation.

* It was helpful to focus on a particular theme, issue, verse, or topic. This created a direction for my ruminations. Otherwise, my mind tended to wander from topic to topic with little active reflection.

❖ Structured prayer worked better than freeform prayer because it kept my mind focused and decreased idle rumination. I often would pray the prayer of *examen*, in which I brought the previous twenty-four hours before God in ways that led to prayer. I found that if the traffic jam ahead needed my attention, after I had negotiated the obstacle I could move back to where I was in the rhythm of that prayer form.

❖ Some days were better than others when it came to freeway prayer. Sometimes the problem was the traffic; at other times it was the pressure of what lay ahead that day; mostly it was my own anxiety, fear, or lack of focus that made prayer difficult. On most days, my focus came and went. I still have a lot to learn. Silent retreats may be the best environment in which to pray, but I can seldom get away to a retreat center. By contrast, the freeway is there every day. It is far, far from an ideal environment, but prayer on the freeway beats not praying at all.

Where are the gaps in your day? How can you fill them? What responses are most appropriate to which gaps? These are questions to consider as you seek to create a prayer plan that fits your life.

WEEKLY EXERCISES
Each day: Use the first four days this week to work through, on your own, the three prayer experiences that you did not do, plus *lectio divina*. Then try summing up what you have been learning about prayer by creating the best way for you to pray on a regular basis.

Day one: Another prayer style. After you complete the prayer exercise, reflect on how easy or difficult it was for you.

Day two: Another prayer style. After you complete the prayer exercise, reflect on how easy or difficult it was for you.

Day three: Another prayer style. After you complete the prayer exercise, reflect on how easy or difficult it was for you.

Day four: Another prayer style. After you complete the prayer exercise, reflect on how easy or difficult it was for you.

Day five: Your prayer style. Ask God to guide you as you reflect on what you have learned about prayer from this course. Based on your experience and your reflection, sketch out what would be a good pattern for you to follow in your daily prayer.

Notes
1. The four human temperaments (as defined by David Keirsey and Marilyn Bates in *Please Understand Me*, Del Mar, CA: Prometheus Nemesis Book Co., 1978, 1984) are derived from the Myers-Briggs type letters.
2. These descriptions are taken from *Prayer and Temperament: Different Prayer Forms for Different Personality Types* by Chester P. Michael and Marie C. Norrisey (Charlottesville, VA: The Open Door, 1984) pp. 21-22. I have made use of the seminal work by Michael and Norrisey throughout this session. This is a fine book to study if you are interested in this topic.
3. Michael and Norrisey, pp. 59-60.
4. Michael and Norrisey, p. 70.
5. This exercise is adapted from an exercise in Michael and Norrisey, p. 54.
6. Michael and Norrisey, p. 76.
7. Michael and Norrisey, p. 82.
8. Roy M. Oswald and Otto Kroeger, *Personality Type and Religious Leadership* (Washington, DC: The Alban Institute, 1989, 1990), p. 93.
9. Michael and Norrisey, p. 88.
10. *Lectio divina* is the subject of *Contemplative Bible Reading* in this series.
11. The *Oxford Book of Prayer*, p. 75.

A SELECT BIBLIOGRAPHY ON PRAYER

Appleton, George, ed. *The Oxford Book of Prayer*. London: Oxford University Press, 1985.

Baillie, John. *A Diary of Private Prayer*. Oxford: Oxford University Press; New York: Charles Scribner's Sons, 1949.

Bloom, Anthony. *Beginning to Pray*. New York: Paulist Press, 1970.

Bockmuehl, Klaus. *Listening to the God Who Speaks*. Colorado Springs, CO: Helmers & Howard, 1990.

Bovet, Theodore. *Have Time and Be Free*. Richmond, VA: John Knox Press, 1964.

Foster, Richard. *Prayer: Finding the Heart's True Home*. San Francisco: HarperSanFrancisco, 1992.

Griffin, Emilie. *Clinging: The Experience of Prayer*. San Francisco: Harper & Row, 1984.

Kaisch, Ken. *Finding God: A Handbook of Christian Meditation*. New York: Paulist Press, 1994, 381 pp.

Kidner, Derek. *Psalms 1-72* and *Psalms 73-150* (The Tyndale Old Testament Commentaries). Downers Grove, IL: InterVarsity Press, 1973, 1975.

Lewis, C. S. *Reflections on the Psalms*. New York: Harcourt, Brace and World, 1958.

Lewis, C. S. *Letters to Malcolm: Chiefly on Prayer*. New York: Harcourt, Brace and World, 1964.

Louf, André. *Teach Us to Pray*. Cambridge, MA: Cowley Publications, 1992.

Nouwen, Henri. *Behold the Beauty of the Lord: Praying with Icons*. Notre Dame, IN: Ave Marie Press, 1987.

Peterson, Eugene. *Answering God*. San Francisco: Harper & Row, 1989.

Postema, Don. *Space for God: The Study and Practice of Prayer & Spirituality*. Grand Rapids: Bible Way, 1983.

Leader's Notes for This Study

Starting a Small Group to Learn Meditative Prayer

All it takes to start a group is the willingness of one person to make some phone calls. When you invite people to consider joining the small group, be sure to explain how the group will operate because this is a different sort of small group. (See "How to Use This Guide" on pages 7-10, which explains the nature of this group.)

The best way to use this material is to do each session in order. However, this will take ten sessions. If your group does not have that much time, there are other options. For example, you could do just the six sessions that examine styles of prayer (sessions 1, 3, 4, 5, 6, and 8) and omit the two that examine the Psalms (sessions 2 and 7).

It is more important to meet in the right sort of place for this small group than for most small groups. The key issue is silence. You cannot pray easily except in a quiet space. This will mean finding a home or a room where children, pets, and the telephone will not interrupt you.

Get enough copies of this book so each person has one. The book contains all the information needed for each of the small group sessions as well as information on the ways of prayer.

The Art of Leadership

It's not difficult to be a small group leader. All you need is

❖ the willingness to lead,
❖ the commitment to read through all of the materials prior to the session,
❖ the sensitivity to others that will allow you to guide the discussion without dominating it, and
❖ the willingness to be used by God as a small group leader.

Here are some basic small group principles that will help you do your job:

Ask the questions: Let group members respond.

Guide the discussion: Ask follow-up questions (or make comments) that draw others into the discussion and keep the discussion going. For example, "John, how would you answer the question?" or "Anybody else have any insights into this question?"

Start and stop on time: If you don't, people may hesitate to come because they never know when they will get home.

Stick to the time allotted to each section: There is always more that can be said in response to any question. It's your job to make sure that the discussion keeps moving from question to question. Remember, it's better to cut off discussion when it's going well than to let it go on until it dies out.

Model answers to questions: Whenever you ask a question to which everyone is expected to respond (for example, an "Open" question as opposed to a Bible study question), you, as leader, should be the first person to respond. In this way you model the right length—and appropriate level—of response.

Understand the intention of different kinds of questions:

❖ *Experience questions*: The aim is to cause people to recall past experiences and share these memories with the group. There are no right or wrong answers to these questions. They facilitate the group process by getting people to share their stories and to think about the topic.

❖ *Forced-choice questions*: Certain questions will be followed by a series of suggested answers (with check-boxes). Generally, there is no "correct" answer. Options aid group members and guide their responses.

❖ *Questions with multiple parts*: Sometimes a question is asked and then various aspects of it are listed below. Ask the group members to answer each of the sub-questions. Their answers, taken together, will answer the initial question.

Introduce each section: This may involve a brief overview of the focus, purpose, and topic of the section plus instructions on how to do the exercise.

Guide the exercises: A major portion of your job will be introducing the exercise. This is the heart of the group experience. Details of how to lead each section will be found below, especially in the material on the first meeting.

Comment: Occasionally bring into the discussion some useful information from your own study. Keep your comments brief. Don't allow yourself to become the "expert" to whom everyone turns for "the right answer."

Notes on Each Session

Before each session, go over the notes for that session. The assumption in this book is that virtually anyone can lead the small group sessions because all the necessary material is contained in this book. However, when a small group leader knows something about the background and intentions of each part of the small group experience, he or she is better able to lead. Hence, these notes provide background material for each session. They do not give "answers" to the questions because most good small group questions do not have a single right answer. They are meant to provoke discussion that will

bring together the collective wisdom of the group. Nor does this section contain "secrets" to which only the leader has access. In fact, group members will be better equipped to participate in the sessions if they take the time to read these notes.

These notes are "front-loaded." That means there are far more notes for session one than for session eight. The general comments about the various parts of the first few sessions apply to all the sessions, and there is no need to repeat them. In subsequent sessions, only the information specific to that session is given.

Timing: Each section of the small group session is labeled with a time range, such as twenty to thirty minutes. The first figure in each range is for groups that are sixty minutes long; the second is for ninety-minute groups. Follow these guidelines carefully. Otherwise you will not have time for the final section of the small group session.

Homework: There are two parts to the work for group members to do on their own.

❖ *Reflection*: In each session on prayer styles there is an essay on some aspect of prayer, often related to the theme of the session. Suggest that people read these on their own. You may decide as a group to read and discuss together these essays.

❖ *Weekly Exercises*: The way to learn to pray is by praying. Group members are encouraged to pray in certain ways during the week between group sessions. You may decide as a group to share insights each week from these exercises.

Session One: Centering Prayer

The first session is most important. During this session those attending will be deciding whether they want to be a part of the group. So your aim as small group leader is to

❖ generate vision about being part of this particular small group (so that each person will want to continue in the group),

❖ give people an overview of the whole course (so they will know where the group is headed),

❖ begin to build relationships (so that a sense of community develops), and

❖ encourage commitment to being a part of the small group (so that everyone will return next week, bringing along a friend!).

A good way to launch the first session of any small group is by eating together prior to the session. Sharing a meal draws people together and breaks down barriers between them. Ask everyone to bring along one dish for the supper. This makes it easy to have a meal for twelve. Or, if you feel ambitious, you might want to invite everyone to dinner at your place. What you serve need not be elaborate. Conversation, not feasting, is the intention of the get-together.

The aim of the meal is to get to know one another in this informal setting. Structure the meal in such a way that a lot of conversation takes place. After the meal, be sure to do the first session completely, not just talk about what you are going to do when the group starts. You want to give everyone the experience of what it would mean to be a part of this small group.

Overview: The overview section provides a road map for the group through the session. Small groups work better when everyone is informed about where the group is going and what steps will be taken to get there. The

more the group knows about what they will be doing together and why, the better they are able to participate. Begin each new small group session with a quick look at the "Overview" so that everybody has a sense of the whole before the session begins.

Begin by welcoming each person to the group. Explain the overall purpose of this small group series using "How to Use This Guide" (and the following "Introduction") on pages 7-14. It is not necessary to go over each point. People can read this section on their own. Just make sure they understand:

❖ The purpose of the series: to learn ways of prayer that go beyond intercession and other more familiar forms of prayer. You can point out the types of prayer that will be covered by looking together at the Contents page.

❖ The details of the sessions: when, where, and for how long you will meet.

❖ The expectations for each group member: full participation, appropriate honesty, and regular attendance. (These details will be discussed more fully in session two when you go over the small group covenant together.)

Make sure the group understands the purpose of the first session: to discuss the mechanics of prayer (using the questionnaire called "A Prayer Inventory", pages 17-18) and learn the process of centering prayer.

End the session overview by leading the group in the unison prayer found in "Overview" (page 15). In each session there will be some sort of prayer with which to begin. You also may want to add prayer of your own after the unison prayer. In subsequent sessions you may wish to ask certain group members to pray after the unison prayer, or you way wish to open the time to spontaneous group prayer.

Open: The aim of this exercise is two-fold: to begin the process of getting to know one another and to begin to think about your experience of prayer and your longings when it comes to prayer. You will notice that in each of the "Open" exercises in this course, the brief introduction ends with a question. This question defines the direction of the exercise and the nature of the sharing together.

Watch the time carefully. It is very easy to spend more than the allotted twenty to thirty minutes on this section because it is such fun sharing stories. However, be sure to end on time. Otherwise you will not get through the rest of the material, which is the heart of the session. Remember that the important thing is not getting through all the questions in the "Open" box. The important thing is inviting each person to speak and beginning to think about prayer together. End this module on time even if you have not covered all of the questions.

Question 1: This is a way to introduce yourselves to one another. Be warned that unless you watch carefully, each person will take too long giving these details. As leader, you answer this question first. Take no more than sixty to ninety seconds for your response. Go around the circle, beginning with yourself, and give each person time to respond (this is called a circle response).

Question 2: This begins to get at the question of motivation for joining a small group such as this. There is no right or wrong answer to this question. Furthermore, people may check more than one box. Again, do not take too

much time. However, give each person a chance to declare publicly his or her longings when it comes to prayer. Again, do this as a circle response in which each person gets to share, beginning with the leader.

Question 3: If you have time, ask people to share brief stories about prayer experiences—their own or that of others. Do not do this as a circle response. Just ask people to share as they wish.

The Mechanics of Prayer: The heart of each small group session is the information and exercises that teach new forms of prayer. In this first session the focus is split between the mechanics of prayer and learning centering prayer.

A Prayer Inventory: Begin by asking people to take a few minutes to fill in the Prayer Inventory. It is not necessary for everyone to finish the whole questionnaire before you begin discussing it. Judge the average amount of time needed by how long it takes you as leader to complete it.

Discuss the questionnaire question by question. The aim in the discussion is not for everyone to share but for the topic to be discussed in helpful ways. Some people will have more experience than others. Others will have more questions than experience. Do this as a group discussion, not as a circle response.

The questions define the mechanics of prayer. You may be surprised at the variety of practices. One of the points you want to make is that there is no one way to pray. Each person has to find his or her own rhythm and style. However, the six questions point out six topics to consider in assessing one's life of prayer.

An Introduction to Centering Prayer: There are various ways to communicate this information to your group. Pick the one that fits best. You can ask people to read the introduction silently to themselves and then ask, "Any questions?" This is the quickest way. Or you can read aloud this material, or summarize it in your own words.

Prayer Exercise: Explain that each person is now going to write his or her own centering prayer with the group's help. Then guide the group step by step through the six steps of the exercise.

❖ Read over the examples of centering prayer either silently or aloud.

❖ Point out the three characteristics of centering prayer.

❖ Guide the brainstorming discussion of the names that can be used and the requests that can be made. Don't let this discussion go on long. Its aim is to get people thinking about options and possibilities.

❖ Now give people time to write a centering prayer.

❖ You may or may not want to take time for each person to share his or her prayer.

❖ The focus of this exercise is the four minutes of silence in which people use the prayers they have written in order to focus in on God. Indicate that you will time the four minutes (silence can feel longer than it is) and conclude by saying, "Amen."

❖ Discuss the experience of centering prayer. Ask people to share what did and did not happen.

Closing Prayer: This will be different in each session depending upon the topic. In the first session, you as leader should be prepared to pray at the end,

committing the whole experience to God and asking that each person will find in the weeks ahead that his or her prayer life is invigorated through this journey together.

Reflection: Point out the use of the "Reflection" in each session. It provides further information about the topic with which the group has worked. Encourage people to read this on their own during the week as a way of deepening their understanding of each form of prayer. Some groups may decide to discuss the "Reflection" during their meetings.

Weekly Exercises: Point these out to the group. These are a way for people to practice on their own what they have learned in the group session. Typically there will be material for use on five days. The benefit of these "Daily Exercises" is that they extend the experience of the small group into the daily life of each group member. This is a good way to deepen one's understanding and experience of prayer. However, these "Daily Exercises" can become a source of guilt. Help people to understand that these are for their use, not enslavement.

Some groups may decide to make the "Daily Exercises" part of their covenant—that is, group members agree to work on these between sessions. The next session might then begin with a check-in time in which each person shares one insight drawn from the "Daily Exercises".

Session Two: Prayer of Blessing

Open: The opening exercise will generally focus on the theme of the session. It does this by taking a low-key, fun look at the theme by inviting group members to tell stories.

There is an alternative way to begin each group session during the weeks to come. You might decide to have group members share what they learned from the prayer exercises during the week between sessions. This is a fine way to check in with each other, and it offers accountability. If people know they will be asked to share about their prayer experience, they are more likely to make time for prayer. Also, this check-in allows group members to learn from one another.

You might decide to mix both exercises, having a few minutes of sharing about the prayer exercise then doing one of the questions in the "Open" section.

The Nature of Blessing: Let the group read this material silently or have someone read it aloud. Its purpose is to introduce and illustrate (from the Bible) the idea of blessing, and then to describe the *berakah*, or prayer of blessing, which will be the focus of the prayer exercise.

Prayer Exercise: Lead this exercise step by step.

1. Ask people to notice the three parts of the *berakah* in the examples given.

2. Do the mini-Bible study of 1 Kings 8 to reinforce the nature and character of this prayer and to get people thinking about how to bless God for who he is and what he has done.

3. Allow people adequate time to write a *berakah*.

Notice the use of sub-groups for prayer. This is a fine way to give people more time for prayer. If your group is large (more than seven people) you might decide to use sub-groups often. I will not always make a point of suggesting sub-groups, but feel free to use them whenever you want to give people more time to interact on a certain exercise. Do not keep the same sub-groups of four each week. Mix up the composition of the sub-groups each time you use them so that the group identity remains with the whole group and not with the sub-group. Rotate the sub-group leadership from week to week.

Bless You: This discussion extends the idea of blessing to the arena of human relationships. This can be a powerful discussion as people realize that they have or have not been blessed.

Session Three: Prayer of Worship
From this point on, notes will only be added when there is a new type of exercise or some special instructions.

Open: This will be a different sort of discussion in that it looks at the question of a small group covenant and not at the experience of group members. It is an important session because a group covenant binds a group together.

Analysis: The aim of this section is to examine the text in such a way that group members will notice what is there and come to understand its meaning. The questions are of two sorts: observation questions that force people to notice the text, and interpretation questions that help them to understand the text. Observation questions do not lend themselves to discussion because people merely state what they notice in order to help one another see what is there. Interpretation questions create more discussion because they require reflection and synthesis of observations.

Question 4: This is an observation question. It is important because it unlocks the structure of the passage: seven imperatives that define the process of worship.

Question 5: This is an interpretation question in that the answer is not drawn directly from the text and so requires reflection. Furthermore, there is not a single "right" answer. The simplest answer is "worship," but people could respond, "prayer," "loving God," "thankfulness," or "praise to God." All of these are different ways to describe the central issue here: coming before God with joy, gladness, gratitude, and praise.

Application: The aim of this section is to make connections between what the group has come to understand the passage to mean and the life issues of each person. Scripture is not meant simply to be understood (though that is crucial); it is meant to be lived out. A small group is a powerful vehicle for helping individuals grasp the personal significance of a text and apply it to their lives.

Questions 7 and 8: These are cluster questions. A central issue is defined and then aspects of that issue are discussed. In question 7 the key issue is the definition of worship found in Psalm 100. Parts b and c of this question seek to help people apply this understanding.

Closing Prayer: End with two kinds of prayer: free prayer and unison prayer using Psalm 100.

❖ *Free Prayer*: The focus of your final prayer together is the praise and worship of God. This will be free prayer (prayer in which all are invited to join in by offering aloud brief prayers in praise of God). If your group is unaccustomed to praying aloud in public, you may want to prepare them for this experience. During the Bible study you can say things like, "Remember what you just said about why you are thankful

to God. You can offer that as a prayer at the end." You might want to give people one or two minutes before the closing prayer to write out what they want to praise God for. As leader, you both begin and end the prayer. As you begin, it is important to model the kind of prayer that is appropriate here. Be brief; be conversational (not liturgical, using special language); be specific (thank God for a particular thing, not for everything in general). It may be helpful if you give the group these instructions before you all pray.

❖ *Unison Prayer*: Move from the free prayer to this prayer by saying, "Let us now pray Psalm 100 together in unison, saying . . ." (and begin the psalm). You may want to pray it together a second time, with even more feeling. Close with, "Amen."

Weekly Exercises: Point these out again, and urge people to take advantage of them, if possible. There are seven exercises (not the usual five) because there are seven aspects of worship that you studied in Psalm 100 and seven other Psalms in the section concluded by Psalm 100.

Background Notes: These can be used by the group during the session itself or read individually afterward. As leader, you will want to go over these several times. They will help you guide the discussion. You may want to refer people to certain notes.

Session Four: Meditative Prayer

Overview: The opening prayer offers yet another way to pray together. It focuses on a passage from Zechariah in which the good news is announced that God is coming and will live among humanity. The advent (or coming) of God is a frequent theme in the Bible: God will come, God has come, God will come again. Invite the group to pray with eager anticipation that God is coming to be in their midst even as they pray. Your task as leader is to:

❖ Give a brief introduction to this type of prayer. Tell them the theme of the passage (see above). Describe the process. You will read the passage twice as they listen for those words or phrases that touch their hearts and draw them to God. There will be a short time for silent reflection (one to two minutes), after which the group members are invited to pray briefly, based on their reflections.

❖ Invite the group to quiet their hearts and minds and to open themselves to the Word of God.

❖ As they sit in silence, with eyes closed, read slowly the passage from Zechariah. Pause. Read it again.

❖ Invite people to meditate in silence (for one to two minutes).

❖ You as leader should break the silence by offering a brief model prayer based on your reflection.

❖ After all who wish to pray have had the opportunity, end the prayer with a short prayer of conclusion.

The Process of Meditative Prayer: Ask people to take two minutes to read this short section. Then go over each of the six parts of the process of meditative prayer. For example, you might begin by saying, "The first step in the process is finding the right story to connect with us. Any comments?" Then move to the second point and talk together about the importance of getting to know a story before imagining yourself a part of it. Do the same sort of thing for each of the six points.

Understanding Meditative Prayer: This is intended to be a discussion. Ask people to read the first point (about the difficulty that some people have in using their imaginations). Invite any comments. Do the same for each of the points. The material is arranged in order of importance to the session. You may not have time to cover every point. (Those who have only one hour for their group will not have time to do this exercise.) Assign the remaining sections as homework.

Session Five: Prayer of *Examen*

Opening Prayer: Don't spend much time on this opening prayer (even though it could go on for some time as the group probes deeper and deeper into the blessings of the past day). There will be more time for such confession of gratitude later in the session. After no more than four or five minutes say, "Let us prayer together the prayer of thanksgiving," and lead the group in the prayer printed on page 53.

Question 1: The sharing provoked by this question could get out of hand if people start long reminiscences. Begin the sharing by modeling a brief answer. The aim of this exercise is to put people back in touch with good memories from the past. They need only name the incident ("Meeting Mary in the tenth grade and finally having a soul-mate to whom I could tell everything"), not describe the details ("Let me tell you how I met Mary . . .").

The Prayer of Examen: This is a longer-than-normal discussion of a prayer style because it is a new way of thinking about prayer for most people, and it is a three-part process.

There are several options for processing this material with the group, discussed below in the order of how long each takes. Remember that in the next part of the exercise, each person will go over a summary of the prayer of *examen* privately as he or she seeks to pray this prayer, so it is not necessary to make sure in this discussion that everybody understands everything.

❖ If people read this material prior to the session (as suggested at the end of session four), then just ask, "Does everybody understand the three steps in the prayer of *examen*?"

❖ Or, if people have not already read the material, let them do so on their own now. It will take under five minutes. Then ask the above question and allow enough discussion to make sure the process of *examen* is understood.

❖ Or, as leader, summarize each section for people as they follow along in the text.

❖ Or, read the section aloud. This is the most time-consuming way to get this material before people.

Session Six: Written Prayers
Why Use Written Prayers?: This is an information section. Make sure the group grasps the two parts: the reasons written prayers are a problem for some people, and the reasons others have used them so successfully in prayer.

Discussion: Follow with a brief discussion that allows group members to express their views on the issue of written prayers. If anyone strongly disagrees with using written prayers, accept this but ask that they stay open throughout the prayer exercise today—open to what God might say to them via the written prayers. You also might want to ask how they have responded to praying psalms aloud (which are written prayers) because the community of God has long practiced this.

Prayer Exercise: Preparation: This exercise is self-explanatory and is similar to others you have done together. It prepares people for "A Service of Prayer" by helping them to see its structure and its basis in the Lord's Prayer. It also allows them to write a prayer to be used in the service.

A Service of Prayer: This will be a longer time of prayer than you normally have. Your discussion should prepare people to pray together. This exercise is the main focus of this group session.

You will lead this service. The printed prayers are to be said in unison. Begin each of these with phrases such as, "Let us confess our dependence on God by praying together" or "Let us prayer together saying. . . ." At those points at which people are to read prayers they have written, pause and allow people to pray. Then move to the next topic. At several points the option is open for free prayer. Invite people to pray aloud at these points with either written or spontaneous prayers.

Depending upon the time available, you may wish to shorten this time of prayer by dropping out some of the printed prayers.

Session Seven: Prayer of Distress
See the discussion under session three for information about how this type of session functions.

Session Eight: Prayer Styles and Personality
Open: The aim of this exercise (apart from allowing people to share a bit more about themselves) is to get the group thinking about personality type. You need to have more of an activist role in this opening exercise than normal. Usually your only job as leader is to ask the question and then be the first to answer it (and so provide a model for how it might be answered). This time you will want to give some input.

Question 1: The way people respond to this question should point to whether they are introverts (I) or extroverts (E). An introvert is a person who, among other things, gets recharged by being alone in silence, reflection, and other inner-directed activities. An extrovert, on the other hand, gets recharged by being with other people. After everyone has a chance to respond, share this fact with the group. You might want to discuss this for a moment.

Question 2: This question gets at a second set of the Myers-Briggs categories: the difference between perceiving types (P) and judging types (J). Perceiving types tend to be more spontaneous. They "let it happen" and "go with the flow." Judging types are more organized. They prefer planning and order. Share this information once everyone has had a chance to respond. By means of the first two questions you have helped people define two of the four Myers-Briggs letters.

Question 3: While it is true that the Myers-Briggs typology has come to be widely used and widely valued, there are people who are (rightly) hesitant about being "defined." This discussion will allow the group to see that such "definitions" are mere pointers, that there is no such thing as a "good" or "preferred" personality type—only different types.

Defining Your Temperament: It should take less than five minutes for people to complete this test. Use it to discuss temperament. Remember that this "test" is merely an indicator of temperament. It is too brief and too limited for it to be anything else. Don't let people read too much into it. You will see its limitation when not everyone checks the same box in each of the three questions.

Prayer Exercise: This exercise is easy to lead. After you finish working through the temperament test, give people the next fifteen to twenty-five minutes (depending on whether you have a total of sixty or ninety minutes for the small group session) to pray on their own. You might want to give people a "two-minute warning" so they can draw their prayer to a close.

Because this is an individual exercise, people might want to scatter throughout the house. The solitude might foster deeper prayer.

Farewell: Because this is the final session in the course, it would be wise to allow some extra time at the end to bring closure to the group experience. Take some time to sum up the experience, to affirm one another, and to plan what is next for your group (if anything).

If you enjoyed MEDITATIVE PRAYER, you'll want to explore the rest of this series as well.

Spiritual disciplines are simply ways to open ourselves to God. They help us become aware of the many ways God speaks to us and provide us with ways to respond. SPIRITUAL FORMATION study guides by Richard Peace explore and explain how the use of disciplines (such as journaling, Bible reading, and prayer) can deepen both our walk with God and our community with other believers. While many think of the spiritual disciplines as solitary pursuits, this series allows group members to share together the riches of a deeper walk with God.

Other Spiritual Formation study guides by Richard Peace include:

Spiritual Journaling
Spiritual Autobiography
Contemplative Bible Reading

NAVPRESS
BRINGING TRUTH TO LIFE